THE VANISHED WORLD

An Autobiography

Illustrated by John Ward

H. E. BATES

LARGE PRINT
Oxford, England

First published in Great Britain 1969
by Michael Joseph Ltd

Published in Large Print 1998 by ISIS Publishing Ltd,
7 Centremead, Osney Mead, Oxford OX2 0ES,
by arrangement with Michael Joseph Ltd

British Library Cataloguing in Publication Data
Bates, H. E. (Herbert Ernest), 1905-1974
   The vanished world. – Large print ed. – (Reminiscence)
   1. Bates, H. E. (Herbert Ernest), 1905-1974 – Biography
   2. Novelists, English – 20th century – Biography 3. Large
   type books
   I. Title
   823.9'12

ISBN 0-7531-5429-3

ISBN 0-7531-5755-1 (pb)

Printed and bound by MPG Books Ltd, Bodmin, Cornwall

CHAPTER
ONE

I was born under Taurus, the Bull, that supposedly most favoured of the signs of the Zodiac, and was further blessed, if Old Wives' tales are to be believed, by being born wrapped in a caul (from O. Eng. Calle, Fr. Cale, a cap), a membranous covering, a portion of the *amnion*, which is sometimes found still enveloping the head of a child after birth. Various superstitions have from earliest times been attached to this caul, called in Scotland *sely how*, a holy or lucky hood, among them being that a child so adorned is exceptionally blessed and gifted, that the caul itself is a sign of good luck and, when preserved, an infallible protection against drowning. For these reasons it was often sold by midwives, more especially to sailors. Indeed I am assured that cauls are still sold by hospital porters in seaports.

It is easy to see why a caul should be considered a protection against drowning, since an infant may well drown at birth with the breaking of its mother's water. It is also no doubt considered lucky because of its rarity. My own doctor in fact assures me he has never seen one in all the years of his practice, though I recently talked to a young district nurse who had seen two cauls in the first year of her practice, much to the envy of several doctors she knew.

In this matter of being born in a caul I was in celebrated company. David Copperfield was born in a caul, as also was Sigmund Freud, back in 1856, in Vienna. The account by Dickens' hero of his birth (the novel appeared six years before Freud was born) is vastly entertaining and vivid, the account of Freud's hardly less interesting. Both confirm what I have already said of the supposedly blessed nature of the phenomenon and this is how Dickens, through the mouth of Copperfield, describes it:

"I was born in a caul, which was advertised for sale, in the newspapers, at the low price of fifteen guineas. Whether sea-going people were short of money at that time, or were short of faith and preferred cork-jackets, I don't know; all I know is, that there was but one solitary bidding, and that was from an attorney connected with the bill-broking business, who offered two pounds in cash, and the balance in sherry, but declined to be guaranteed from drowning on any higher bargain. Consequently the advertisement was withdrawn at a dead loss . . . and ten years afterwards the caul was put up in a raffle down in our part of the country, to fifty members at half a crown a head, the winner to spend five shillings. The caul was finally won by an old lady who paid all of her five shillings in halfpence and "was never drowned, but died triumphantly in bed, at ninety-two." Her caul was therefore remarkably cheap, especially in view of the fact that she was anyway tuppence ha'penny

2

short in payment, though in fact the price of cauls had sunk as low as thirty shillings by the end of the century.

Jews in Russia and Poland maintain that it is lucky "to be born in a little shirt", a belief that seems certainly to have been connected with Freud, himself a Jew, whose caul "was believed to ensure him future happiness and fame", and certainly his mother was delighted when later told by an old woman in a pastry shop "that she had brought a great man into the world", an idea that Freud himself discounted, though he was not unimpressed by a still later prophecy, made by an improvising poet in a restaurant, that "I should probably one day become a 'Minister'." This same prophecy, happily unfulfilled, was also made by my maternal grandfather about me and was probably one equally cherished by my father though in his case the wish related to the Church rather than to the Crown. Perhaps another prophecy, contending that those born in a caul are lucky in love, was nearer the mark. Swift, in *Polite Conversations* (1738), wrote "I believe you were born with a caul on your head you are such a favourite among the ladies," and a character in Thomas Randolph's *The Jealous Lover* (1632) declared "Sure I was born with a caul on my head and wrapped in my mother's smock, the ladies do love me so ." There is still further proof of the just esteem in which cauls were held in the fact that there may still be found, in antique shops, heart-shaped lockets, of silver, in which a caul could be kept, the lockets apparently being worn around the neck like a crucifix.

Whether it is in fact lucky to be born in a caul, or as the French say, "*être né coiffé*," or not, it is certain that

I was born, in 1905, into a world of leather and shoe-makers. My grandfather on my mother's side was a shoemaker; my father was also a shoemaker, though not in the sense my grandfather was; my grandfather on my father's side had his own boot and shoe-making business, from which he not infrequently slipped away to the smoother, easier, more seductive life of warmer climates, notably the Mediterranean and later, perman-ently, to Australia; my mother went to work as a half-timer, in the shoe-making industry at the tender age of ten, tying knots, for the princely sum of two shillings a week. If indeed I ever suffer from some ailment of the lungs it may well be because the distant pungent odours of leather and shoemakers' shops still linger tenaciously within me.

Of my two grandfathers I knew the paternal one scarcely at all, except by reputation. I have no personal visual recollection of him whatever, except from photographs, in which he looks remarkably like H. G. Wells, whose undeniable and fatal attraction for women he shared. Short and not particularly handsome, he may fairly be called a lady killer, having caused my father's mother, a beautiful, proud, highly sensitive girl devoted to the world of nature, to die of a broken heart — literally — at the age of twenty-one. That he omitted to marry her was responsible for the fact that, in due course, twentieth-century English literature was spared the em-barrassment of having yet another Herbert Lawrence on the scene. I think I saw him perhaps twice or three times in my life, so frequent and prolonged were his journeys about the world, and on neither occasion did he offer a word or sign of recognition. By contrast I grew up, as I shall presently explain in greater detail, in my maternal grandfather's pocket, bonded in a great warm mutual affection, neither of us able in the other's eyes to do the slightest wrong.

When I say that my maternal grandfather was a shoemaker I mean that he could, after the fashion and tradition of centuries, create a boot or shoe from the sole upwards, stabbing and stitching, with his own hands. The world in which he plied his craft — he used to recall for me an occasion when a messenger rode on a white horse into the little market square of his native Higham Ferrers to bring the news, weeks after the event, that the Crimean War was over — knew no machines for shoemaking, except perhaps treadle-machines for stitching uppers. Consequently I am able still to see him to perfection in the mind's eye: shoemaker's last between his knees, tossing handfuls of tacks and sprigs into his mouth, to my extreme consternation; his awls, thread, leather, files, hammers all about him.

Not only, however, was he a shoemaker, but a craftsman of the highest class: so much so that when very special orders came down from London it was almost always to George William Lucas that they were given. It used to be his proud boast — though boast is altogether too strong a word to apply to so self-effacing, modest a man — let us say therefore that he was proud to have made both the largest and the smallest shoes in the world — the largest being those flat comic seven-league boots worn by the Victorian comedian Little Tich, the smallest a pair of doll-like miniatures for a midget dancer.

Higham Ferrers is a pleasant little stone built town overlooking the serene pastures of the Nene Valley in Northamptonshire. In my boyhood some of its streets were still cobbled. It is not only very nearly plumb in the middle of England, but if you take a pair of compasses and draw a circle of fifty or sixty miles with the little borough as its centre you will find yourself enriched by a truly remarkable company of famous men. Henry V's famous archbishop — of whom more in a moment — was born in the town itself; Thomas Rudd, Charles the First's chief engineer in the Civil War, was also born there; seven or eight miles away the tiny village of Aldwinkle, which has two churches and therefore two rectories, produced within five years John Dryden from one rectory and Thomas Fuller, the historian, from the other; a dozen miles or so to the south, over into Bedfordshire John Bunyan wrote *Pilgrim's Progress* and occasionally came to preach at Higham Ferrers and also at the stone Baptist meeting house which still stands at the end of the street in Rushden where I grew up as a boy; another dozen miles over the border into Buckinghamshire lived the poet William Cowper; Shakespeare and Milton just about squeeze into the perimeter; farther down the valley John Clare wrote his poems, later to die in the asylum at Northampton, farther up the valley. This indeed is the old Kingdom of Mercia, cradle of so much of our literature and of the Standard English we know.

At one time Higham Ferrers was to have been a university town. Indeed its main street is still called College Street, in which stand the partially restored buildings of the college itself, with its associations with

All Souls College, Oxford. These buildings, half in decay, were part of a farm in my boyhood and it was here, from time to time, that my grandfather and I went through a mystical process known as "tekking the old gal down." This was the business of taking the sow to the boar, though my innocence never grasped what the process exactly consisted of. This sow was a remarkable lady. Small and puny when a suckling — what is sometimes called a dillin — she grew up to be bountiful both in girth and fertility. Great pink belly swaying, her keyboard of teats swinging, her ponderous, passive mouth slightly slobbering, she would of necessity have to be coaxed, rather than driven, the two miles or so from sty to farm. The resulting fruitfulness of her life was truly prodigious. First she began with modest litters of ten or a dozen; then fourteen and fifteen; then seventeen and eighteen; then an incredible nineteen. With bated expectancy we awaited her crowning twenty. Alas, it never came and soon she was hanging in the form of salty pictures, vast, fatty, succulent sides of bacon, on the walls of my grandmother's kitchen.

My grandfather was greatly given to story-telling, in the pursuit of which he almost invariably began at the end of the story and worked backwards to the beginning, clearly on the assumption that you already knew what the beginning was. Until you were familiar with this method you were bound to be enmeshed in much confusion. Thus it was that occasionally, as we were driving the horse and trap along the motorless summer lanes outside the town, he would pull up the horse, point the whip across the fields and say with solemn and mysterious emphasis: "Masterpiece of man. Plough-boy. Used to scare the crows down there."

Who this masterpiece of a man was it was utterly impossible to tell until, perhaps half a mile further on, you were presented with the cryptic enlightenment of the single word "Chichele", followed at about the same interval by "Archbishop" and at a third pause by "Plough-boy". Now my grandfather had, in mid-Victorian times, also been a plough-boy, scaring crows and taking his place as a boy of six every morning at four o'clock in the big farm kitchen a stone's-throw from the house where he was born, there to be given, together with all other farm-hands, a pint of beer. He could never manage to drink this beer — pretty strong it must have been, brewed as it was in the farm's own brew 'us — though there was never any lack of willing lips and throats to help him out in that direction.

It thus became borne upon me that the masterpiece of a man, Henry V's great archbishop at the time of Agincourt, who also has a part in Shakespeare's play and whose tomb may now be seen in Canterbury Cathedral in company with the Black Prince and Thomas a'Beckett, had served as plough-boy and crow-scarer side by side with my grandfather. It was not for some considerable time that I amazedly discovered that some six hundred years separated the two local plough-boys. Not that this had the remotest effect on the great, glowing fraternal pride with which my grandfather always spoke of Chichele, a pride he also devoted to the great Mr Gladstone, of whom he was also accustomed to speak as if Victoria's Prime Minister and himself were near relations.

Chichele was in fact born in 1364, the son of Thomas Chichele, a farmer and Mayor of the borough. There were two other sons, Robert, afterwards Sir Robert, who became prosperous in the city of London and a great friend of the famed Dick Whittington; and William, who became a Sheriff in the city in 1410 and later an Alderman. Distinguished though the brothers must have been it was Henry who caught the eye of no less a person than William de Wykeham, Bishop of Winchester, when on a visit to the town. As a result Henry was placed at Winchester School and his extraordinarily distinguished and fruitful career was launched. Promotion to the Archdeaconry of Salisbury came in 1408; a little later he was sent by Henry IV as ambassador to Pope Gregory and then to the council of Pisa in 1409. In 1413 he was made Archbishop of Canterbury and in 1414 Henry V sent him as ambassador to Charles I of France and John, Duke of Burgundy.

If the world of my childhood, like that of grandfather, is almost wholly a vanished one, it is pleasant to record that that of Chichele still survives today in the shape of two splendid buildings of his own creation, both in the shadow of the magnificent church of Higham Ferrers: first the delicate and enchanting little grammar school in Perpendicular style, secondly the larger and altogether heavier-looking Bede-House, created as an institution and almshouse — rather oddly, I always feel — for twelve men and one woman. The men selected for this benefaction were entitled to wear a scarlet star on their coats and it was, I think, the proudest day of my grandfather's life when, six hundred years after these two fine buildings were erected, he too could walk in his native town so star-adorned while I, from time to time, changed into my football kit in the empty, slightly sepulchral Bede-House itself.

But before this happened there fell on the craft of shoe-making, about 1910, a great blight. The day of the hand-craftsman was virtually over; the machine was inexorably advancing. As in the Swiss watch-making industry so in the world of shoe-making almost all the work was done at home. There were no forty-hour weeks, no clocking in. For ever independent, shoemakers were a law unto themselves, mostly getting rousing drunk on Saturdays and Sundays, never by long tradition working on Mondays. Either out of duty to their patron saint St Crispin or in pursuit of a cure for mountainous hangovers, they sought solace in the surrounding countryside, rabbiting, coursing, mushrooming, following hounds, walking or riding miles by devious routes to secret hide-outs where bare-fisted bruisers bloodily battered themselves to pulp before crowds of gentry and poor alike. With Monday behind them, shoemakers returned to their lasts, madly stitching and hammering away until midnight and even into the small hours in pursuit of cash that would, when Saturday came again, be riotously squandered on booze and the "blues".

Into the hay-fields of June and the harvest-fields of August they also went, to join "you sun-burnt sickle-men of August weary", mostly the great gangs of itinerant Irish labourers who had been seasonally invading England ever since Stuart times. They too were roughly, fiercely independent. The communal bargain struck with the local farmer for the reaping of wheat, oats and barley was based solely on beer and money and if the bargain had to be gilded in favour of the reaper it was always by means of more beer, potently home-brewed of course. Years later a smallish man of cunning appearance with the appropriate nick-name of Smack used to lend my grandfather a hand at harvest time, a magnificent and devastating craftsman with the scythe who confessed that he and his father thought little or nothing of drinking, in hay-field or harvest-field, twenty-five pints a day. His thirst remaining un-diminished, I therefore often found myself riding pony-back to the outdoor beer-house, to bring back a load of bottles in a nose-bag in readiness for dinner-time.

All pubs and beer-houses also sold, in those days, small beer; which, though not strong enough for men, had body enough for boys or what in Northamptonshire were vividly described as "bwoy-chaps", the word boy always being pronounced in that strong, special, earthy way. Old women also brewed, and were still brewing in my boyhood, a herb beer, confined solely to summer, made of nettles — I rather fancy the stingless, flowering kind — dandelions, root ginger and various other wild hedgerow plants, together with yeast and sugar. It had a mildly astringent taste, not unlike a watered-down vermouth, and was known, as near as it is possible to get the pronunciation into words, as diar-drink or dior-drink. This curious word, which I always imagined to be strictly local, has had me infinitely puzzled for a great many years and it was only recently that I discovered that the Welsh name for herb beer, the brew being composed of exactly the same ingredients as the Northamptonshire one, is *diod-dail*: hence, it would clearly seem, the diod-drink, or herb drink, of my boyhood. English dictionaries offer no clues as to the word *diod* and perhaps only some erudite modern Professor Higgins can explain for us how this Welsh word came to have common usage in Midland England.

I would gravely doubt if diod-drink is ever made today, or for that matter sloe-gin or blackberry-vinegar, a concoction of hideous, indeed almost brutal throat-searing flavour once made and kept by every North-amptonshire household as a sovereign remedy, like eucalyptus and camphorated oil, against the barking coughs of winter. I should doubt also if the milkman of today, in his sterilized world of huge dairy combines, ever delivers beastings or bustings or biznins, as we always called them: the first milk given by the cow after calving. But beastings, or biznins were, in our world, little short of a luxury. The extreme richness of the milk cooked quickly into a custard that was creamy, stiff and rich. It was always a red letter day when the biznins arrived and I loved it.

This world, in which hiring-fairs were still a common autumnal practice and *largesse* was still distributed as it had been from time immemorial, all of it I fancy little changed since Shakespeare's day, also belonged to the women. They too invaded the fields of hay at harvest, their children with them, the children to make bonds for the sheaves, the women to bond and stook them. I have heard my grandfather say of these women that it was no uncommon sight to see a woman suddenly unbutton her blouse in the harvest-field, take out a milky breast, and suckle a child old enough and tall enough to stand and reach the nipple. Later they fell on the stook-empty fields like flocks of human hens, in the guise of gleaners, gleaning frenziedly from dawn to dark, when the final gleaning bell sounded: a custom so rewarding that I have heard my paternal great-grandmother, who brought up her twelve children on twelve shillings a week supplemented by a further half-crown earned by her husband as town lamplighter, say that on one occasion she and her family gleaned enough corn to justify hiring a threshing machine.

If the world of the gleaner, a figure common to the summer scene ever since Ruth stood in tears among the alien corn, was to continue for some good few years yet, the old world of the handcraft shoemaker was rapidly withering before the blight. The years about 1910 were a time of much distress. Whole families emigrated to Australia and the New World (you could then get a one-way passage for as little as £6); shoemakers went to London in marches of hunger and protest; there were empty houses everywhere. For the shoemaker, the hand craftsman, there was no future.

It was about this time that my grandfather decided to return to the land that had first nurtured him. Stimulated perhaps by that smooth slogan "two acres and a cow" he decided, with two or three of his shopmates, to set up as a small-holder. From a chosen field of about twelve acres, overlooking the great pastoral width of the Nene valley, his share was five. Many years later I met a farmer who well remembered the choice. "They chose it," he said and sadly shook his head, "because in the previous summer it had borne a splendid crop of wheat. They couldn't have chosen worse." The land in fact was wickedly heavy, impossible to touch in winter, drying out to a surface of cracked concrete in summer, a devilish challenge, year in, year out, to a virtually single-handed man.

But if the choice almost meant a sentence of penal servitude for my grandfather for the rest of his life it afforded me the foundation on which all the joys of my childhood, together with all my feeling and love of the countryside, is based. There sprang up for me, out of this very ordinary, unprepossessing piece of Midland earth, a paradise that remains to this day utterly unblemished, a joy for ever.

CHAPTER
TWO

At first the tools my grandfather had for the tillage of this intractable piece of land were pathetically simple. He had neither horse nor stable to put one in. His only vehicle was a wheelbarrow, in which I can distinctly remember being wheeled to the land on spring and summer mornings.

But soon things began to improve and it was largely my father who brought about the improvement. One of the positively good things he had inherited from his recalcitrant father, and which in turn I have failed to inherit from him, was a near genius for doing anything with hammer, saw and nails. Accordingly he began, on Saturday afternoons, to build for my grandfather a few simple farm buildings: a stable, a hen-house, pig-sties, a cart-shed, an out-house for storing tools, seeds and bran for pig-swill, a copper house for boiling potatoes for the pigs, and a privy. There was also a little shed containing a chaff-cutter, the big handle of which I sometimes used to turn on winter afternoons, when I also helped chop up mangelwurzels (wezzles, as they were always called) for horse-feed. The resulting farmyard, later adorned with hay and straw ricks, became the hub of my world.

Soon a succession of horses, some of them no more

than ponies, inhabited the stable. One by one, with disconcerting frequency, they fell down dead. Since their unremitting task was to draw plough, harrow, seed-drill, horse-hoe, trap and a truck from which we sold vegetables, fruit and flowers from house to house two mornings a week, this was by no means surprising. It is in fact astounding that the tumbril from the knacker's yard didn't appear more frequently than it did, to take away its melancholy load of stiffening horse-flesh.

What this continuing succession of tragedies meant to my grandfather, poor and single-handed as he was, I was too young to tell. Small wonder that his figure, once tall and upright, was now deeply bent, or that his hair, black in early manhood, was now completely snow-white. But if I was too young to understand it is equally certain that I was, to him, an intense source of joy and comfort. He had in fact greeted my birth with the words: "Capital! We've had enough o' gals!" — this resounding comment referring not to the fact that he had fathered a whole regiment of women but merely to my mother and her sister, his only children, and even they separated by ten years or so. He had long wanted a son and this, at last, was what I virtually was to him.

If I was also a source of great irritation to him — and I am perfectly certain I was, constant as I was in my cajoling insistence that he take me fishing, birds' nesting, playing cricket or gathering water-cress — he never once revealed it. His sharpest rebuke, not often repeated at that, was a mere "Drop it, boy," though very occasionally he might go so far as to refer to me as "that young gallus". His constant reward for this great indulgence was to be told by my grandmother and aunt that "you'd cut off your head and give it to him if he as much as asked for it," an undoubted truth if ever there was one.

Apart from the main holding with its little farmyard my grandfather rented from time to time two other fields, both pasture and both of about five acres in area, one for the purpose of gathering a stack of hay, the other for grazing one of the unfortunate ponies; but it was really about the little farmyard, with its clucking hens and squealing pigs, that the horizon of my world extended. The crest of the valley here is quite high, wide and open to every searing, soaking wind. On a really clear fine day it was possible here to pick out no less than nine of the church spires for which Northamptonshire is justly famous. Few trees and no great woodlands were there to break the view. Ash, hawthorn and elm, with here and there a few small oaks, made up the general pattern of trees; the beeches, sweet chestnuts, turkey oaks and whitebeams which I now know and love in the south country were never to be seen.

Nevertheless, sparsely clothed as it was, the land in spring and summer was a great thrilling palpitation of bird song. I can see now huge droves of grey elephantine April cloud-shadows rushing across the valley before the western wind and feel the cut of ice in the air each time the sun went in. Along the headlands flowered yellow drifts of coltsfoot, doubly precious because this was a countryside with no primroses, no bluebells, no kingcups, none of Shakespeare's beloved lady-smocks, still to me one of the high aristocrats of England's spring flowers. Above it all a pee-witting chorus of plovers would beat strongly at the air, but never strongly enough to drown the celestial choirs of skylarks, for whose nests I was constantly going in diligent search along the plough furrows. Kestrels hovered above too, poised for the long darting kill, and the May hedgerows clinked with the pink-pink of chaffinches, not long since one of England's commonest birds but now, alas, almost a rarity. And then in summer the yellow hammers, the endless drowsy repetition of "a little bit of bread and no cheese", and the occasional whistle of swan wings beating up from the river.

If my grandfather had no time to come with me birds'-nesting — and how he ever found the time I cannot think — I had perforce to go alone, at first tremulous of being found trespassing in other people's fields, then so lost in the search for nests and eggs that presently I even forgot my fears. The blue clutches of hedge-sparrow and thrush, the green-blue of blackbird, the peppered delicacies of the finches, the scribble of writing-larks, even sometimes the thrill of a plover and the even greater thrill of that marvel among nests, the long-tailed tit, "the pudden-bag": all were part of a nervous spring-time miracle. And sometimes on early mornings, while I still slept, my grandfather would come back to the house, having been up since four o'clock, with a handful of partridge eggs for my breakfast. I can still see them dancing and bubbling, tiny, golden and white, among slices of home-cured bacon in the frying pan.

Of wider journeyings into the surrounding countryside, sometimes into Huntingdonshire, more often into Bedfordshire, to which I looked forward passionately, I shall have much to say later; but often we had shorter journeys to make, either in trap or truck, and the most frequent of these was into the village of Chelveston-cum-Caldicott down the hill, where a little tributary of the Nene twice made a watersplash across the road, white in summer with water ranunculus, green with brook-lime and cress and alive with gudgeon and sticklebacks. Here we always stopped to water the ponies and, in drought years, to fill barrels with water before going on to the village to find out if the cunning and redoubtable Smack could come and knock an acre or two of wheat down or to see some other man about something or other.

Thousands of American ex-servicemen will have no need to be told what and where Chelveston is. Here, after Pearl Harbour, came the bulldozers and bombers to carry out the necessary ruthless murder of part of my childhood countryside. Here, in place of woods where I had gathered violets and revelled in the heady perfume of crowds of cream-green butterfly orchids, there sprang up a vast air-field, furnished with what was probably the most useless and vulnerable flying machine ever sent, like a ponderous duck, into combat: the Flying Fortress. Over-armoured, slow, unable to be fitted with exhaust-cowlings because of the extra weight, it fell prey to Goering's Luftwaffe fighters with an ease so fearful that its first concerted daylight raid over Germany was nothing but naked ruthless murder itself, leaving strong

men weeping at Chelveston and the air-field itself crushed and stunned in mourning.

But of course on those other mornings, as I turned the stones of the brook for the sight of sticklebacks, I had no idea of these things. Every morning was golden; even the First World War had not begun. The hedgerows of spring were clothed with the cream of May-blossom; those of June and July with pink and white dog-roses, meadowsweet and willow-herb. If the paradise made by it all was about to be shattered, not once but twice, I happily hadn't even the remotest suspicion of the gathering cloud. Sticklebacks were in the brook, cuckoos called from the elms, yellowhammers swooned away long summer afternoons in lanes shimmering with heat and virtually undefiled by the motor-car, and consequently all was right with the world.

At the boundary of Chelveston my grandfather would frequently halt the trap to make another of his mysterious "masterpiece of a man" pronouncements. As with Chichele this followed a pattern of cryptic brevity, "the masterpiece" opening being succeeded, a minute or so later, by "coalman", a little later by "musician", then by "London" and finally by "Britton". As a child I had not the faintest idea of what all this meant and it took several years of adult detective work to discover that my grandfather was in fact referring to yet another celebrated son of Northamptonshire, namely Thomas Britton (1644-1714) coalman indeed, musician, book-collector, close acquaintance of nobility and friend of Handel.

The pronouncement on Britton was undoubtedly made

at the parish boundary of Chelveston on the supposition that he was born there, almost every other family in the village being called, even in my time, Britton. In this my grandfather may or may not have been mistaken. *The Dictionary of National Biography* gives Britton's birthplace either as Wellingborough or Higham Ferrers; *Grove's Dictionary of Music* settles for my own birthplace, Rushden. Whichever is correct it is certain that Britton went to London at an early age, apprenticed himself to a coal-merchant in Clerkenwell for seven years and then set up in business for himself, hiring an old stable for the purpose.

This stable was evidently so small as to be described as "not much higher than a Canary Pipe and the window of his State Room but very little bigger than the Bunghole of a Cask". Nevertheless here, in 1678, Britton started his celebrated series of musical *soirées*. These attracted not only some of the most gifted musicians of the time, including the great Handel himself, who played the organ, but leaders of fashion and nobility. Coffee was served at a penny a cup and there were, it seems, "many notable performances in the charming science of Musick".

Music, however, was not the only science in which Britton was interested. He also took up chemistry, turning later to the occult sciences, on which he collected a large and distinguished library. In pursuit of this he was aided by a number of notable and titled bibliophiles, among them the Earl of Oxford, the Duke of Devonshire and the Earls of Pembroke, Winchelsea and Sunderland. All the time he continued to sell coal in the streets. The suspicion that a man of such humble origins could hardly move in elevated circles without nefarious purposes of some kind led to his being variously accused of being an atheist, a Jesuit, a Presbyterian and a magician. Grove declares all of this to be quite unfounded — "Britton was a plain, simple, honest man." But one thing seems to have been certain: he was highly superstitious, a fact that seems to have led, in 1714, to his death. To one of the concerts came a celebrated ventriloquist, a blacksmith named Honeyman, who proceeded to tease Britton by telling him that unless he at once fell on his knees and repeated the Lord's Prayer he would die within an hour or two. The wretched Britton immediately did as he was told but was apparently so frightened that he died a few days later. His collection of some fourteen hundred books was auctioned after his death and the catalogue of it is still, apparently, extant.

These "masterpiece of a man" episodes are by no means irrelevant. Indeed they throw much light on my grandfather's considerable character. It must be remembered that the only schooling he ever received was a very brief period at a mid-Victorian Dame school, so that although he could read a little he could scarcely write his name. Yet he was a man of advanced and liberal views, constantly energetic in politics, perpetually scornful of and in opposition to all organised religion, a co-founder of the local co-operative society and above all a staunch and passionate Englishman. His face, bronzed by wind and sun, with its fine aquiline nose and pure white hair, had about it an indisputably aristocratic air. What even a smattering of education would have done for him is something I often ask myself and it is my friend David Garnett, I think, in the first volume of his own autobiography, *The Golden Echo*, who touches on the answer.

"We have reason to believe," he says, "that every living creature is a fresh permutation of ancestral genes which determines its individuality. Half of the possible genes are passed on to the new individual from each parent, half are discarded. The hereditary constitution which results is infinitely more important than education or experience."

Precisely; so with my grandfather.

CHAPTER
THREE

The church of Higham Ferrers, thanks no doubt to the early influence of Chichele, has always been, and still is, very High; that at Rushden always has been, and still is, very Low. My grandfather would have no part of this High Church, nor indeed of any Low one. Scornfully he spoke of "Popery and humbug, sciencing about with incense and singing in nightshirts". My father, by contrast, was a deeply religious man, not merely devoted to the Methodist faith but positively locked in its uncompromising strait-jacket. It is therefore time now to say something of him, the other great formative influence on my childhood.

He started life with several disadvantages, not to say misfortunes the most grievous of which was the death of his broken-hearted mother when he was two, followed shortly afterwards by that of his grandmother, in whose care he had been left. The death of his mother was, I think, something that secretly grieved him for the rest of his life. In photographs she is shown as a proud, very beautiful girl in that pure mould for which the Midland valleys of England are justly famous. Not only are the people of these valleys, from Ouse to Trent, the best looking in all England; they are probably some of the handsomest in all Europe. Both my father and mother were cast in this mould and if family gossip is to be accepted there was a succession, on the Lucas side, in Victorian times, of such beauties as to keep squires, doctors and young bloods constantly on the boil.

My father's mother, as I have already said, cared passionately for the countryside, as indeed all of that side of the family did. My father, and indeed I in turn, inherited this strong love of nature and in my father's case it was responsible for some interesting tricks on his part. Sent to the local board school, he quickly discovered that the nearby National school, or church school, was favoured with several more days' holiday, on such occasions for instance as Ascension Day, than his own. Apart from playing truant pretty often anyway, he therefore from time to time did a quick change act, removing his allegiance from Board School to National, where he enjoyed the bonus holiday before going back again.

At the age of ten he went, like my mother, to work. Those were the days of half-timers, when children of ten went to school for one half of the day and to work for the other. The hand shoemakers of the day also employed small boys — at, I should guess, about sixpence a week — as runners between their back-yard shops and factories. They were known as sweaters. My father was never a sweater but I should guess that his starting wage was not more than three or four shillings a week. It is certain that my mother's was only two.

In spite of all this and in spite of much truancy and changes of scholastic scene, he had achieved such distinction at the age of thirteen, then the school-leaving age, that he was asked to stay on as a teacher. This invitation he declined. He had in fact an excellent and diligent brain. He could write a beautiful copper-plate hand, though for all ordinary purposes he used a sort of secondary copperplate, quite excellent in itself. He was an extremely good mathematician; in all my experience I never knew him to make a spelling mistake; his grasp of general knowledge was wide and first class; he read a good deal and collected himself a tolerably good little library.

His other great passion was music. Orphaned, pitched into work at childhood in an industry he hated, virtually abandoned by a profligate father who gaily gave up his partnership in business to go to Australia, largely on the grounds of ill-health, though he lived to his mid-eighties, my father nevertheless applied his difficult adolescence first of all to teaching himself to read music, then to buying himself a piano. He himself was possessed of a very fine, strong bass voice, the rich warm depth of which I can still hear emerging from the tiers of the chapel choir, of which he was subsequently conductor, like a splendid diapason.

His was the age of male-voice choirs, male-voice quartettes and mixed quartettes and he threw himself into all this sort of thing with much conscientious and ardent activity. I do not wish to give the impression here that he was in any way a narrow-minded or bigoted man — this indeed was far from the case — but the strictness with which he devoted himself to the Methodist faith was, to say the least of it, pretty unyielding. It is hard to say whether pubs or clubs inspired him to greater contempt. Card-playing, gambling, horse-racing, drinking, dancing: all, in the true tradition of Wesley, were anathema to him, the only exception being that he enjoyed a game of cribbage. Even there the eye of the faith was for ever watchful, as I discovered some years after I had married when I remarked, after he had enjoyed a phenomenal run of luck on the crib board, that he was having the luck of the very devil himself. He at once fell upon me with righteous wrath, as if I were still a recalcitrant small boy who had done something phenomenally disgraceful. After the same fashion he would suddenly rise from his seat at a football match to deliver a loud and stern homily to some spectator who had just counselled the referee to keep "his bleeding eyes open". What he would have said about today's so-called permissive society, where tons of toilet paper are thrown at goal-keepers every season and the literary advisor of the National Theatre uses the language of gutter-snipes on television I simply dare not think.

One result of all this was that I grew up in an atmosphere of intense respectability in which, though we were never affluent, we knew nothing of the poverty and squalor so common to Edwardian working class towns, where booze and the pawnshop dominated a great part of the population. My parents were never a farthing in debt; great was the pride they took, as my grandparents did, in paying their way. Yet the margin left between one pay packet and another was often as low as sixpence, as manifested by a story of my mother's in which she tells of being left with exactly that sum of a Friday morning, faced with the problem of giving my father the hot midday meal a working man expected in those days. Quite undeterred, she crossed the road to the butcher's shop, bought a pennyworth of suet, two pennyworth of kidney and three pennyworth of steak and then went back to make a steak-and-kidney pudding, her purse empty.

My father pursued his passion for nature and the countryside, and incidentally fostered my own, by doing a vast amount of walking — oh! how we walked. Winter and summer we tramped, by Shanks's Pony, the bus-less, motor-less roads, the footpaths, the blackberry hedges, the river tow-paths, the woodland ridings, mostly in Bedfordshire, my father striding out athletically, I desperately struggling to keep up. I vividly recall an occasion when — I was not more than five — we penetrated deep by footpath into the next county, lost our way and at last, after hours of wandering, came to a sign-post indicating that it was still six miles to home. Even my father afterwards confessed to dismay.

To this day the joy of these walks remains. There is a certain woodland just over the Bedfordshire border that is crossed by a broad grass riding which is etched on my mind with such imperishable clarity that I can still see and smell the bluebells, the honeysuckle, the meadow-sweet, the dog roses and the sheer concentrated fragrance of summer leaf and sap. If I have nothing else to thank my father for — and I have a very great deal — this in itself would be enough.

Not that we always walked. Quite often, mostly when my father's choir or quartette was off to keep an

engagement to sing at some village fête or chapel or garden party or great house, we went by brake or wagonette. The scene is as remote as something out of Pickwick or Hardy's *The Woodlanders*: the varnished brake itself, the gleaming brass and neats-foot oil of the harness, the odours of horse-flesh and horse-droppings, the summer dust, the harsh crunch of metal wheel rims on the rough stones of the road, the pantomime of half the passengers having to alight at the approach of every modest hill — and above all an air of unsophisticated, almost naïve enjoyment that our contemporary world of fast cars, planes, television and vast motorways never knows and will never know: a vanished world indeed.

It is undoubtedly from those summer journeyings that my adult preoccupation with great country houses, in terms of much of my fiction, stems. Rich though Northamptonshire is in great and lovely houses it is more the transition from redbrick, factory and chapel to the broad serenity and dignity of noble estates that, I fancy, has left so imperishable an impression on me. I still re-experience the feeling, fifty years later, that the start of these journeys was very like being let out of prison.

In structure Rushden is an odd town; in the lateness and rapidity of its development perhaps odder still. Unlike Higham Ferrers it has no ancient history worthy of the name. At the beginning of the 19th century it was still a mere village of a few hundred inhabitants; by the end of the century it had become an industrial town of 15,000 people. Its shape ill-suited to bear the scars of jerry-building and the Industrial Revolution, might well have been carved out by a madman gone slightly berserk with a giant bulldozer. It is impossible to get out of the town without going uphill. Hills rise and slant and dive in all directions, some so precipitously that one or two streets are closed to downhill traffic. The miserable little brook that runs through the entire length of it seems to be the central point of magnetism for these many steep streets and alley-ways, which can be wickedly cold in winter and steamily, oppressively hot in summer. The only buildings of any architectural significance in the whole town are the church, with its famous Strainer arch, one of only three in England, and the Hall, which is the setting for a great deal of my novel, *Love for Lydia*. The rest is a palpably dreadful mess of that mixture of blue slate, factory, chapel and that harsh Midland red brick which equally oppresses heart, soul, eye and senses.

Just occasionally you find this dreary pattern relieved by corner facings of that deep beer-brown ironstone which lies near the surface of the Nene and Walland Valleys, and sometimes in the years of my boyhood you would find grapevines growing on the south walls of these older, softer houses of local stone. But the street in which I was born was wholly of brick, not all red but ranging from plain white at the southern, more respectable end to a shade of dreary dreadful puce-blue at the other. In it were two boot factories, and next to one of them I was born. In the street running in at right angles almost opposite to my parents' house stood the factory where my father worked, and immediately over the roof of the pork butcher's opposite us I could see, on winter evenings, the gas-lights of another factory shining greasy-yellow until six o'clock. The geography of the town might indeed have been laid out by some shoe-making dictator who had insisted that for every hundred yards of dwelling houses there should be thirty or forty of factory sandwiched between and then had added the humanitarian proviso that a bake-house and a chapel or two should somehow be tucked in among them. Immediately opposite us there were indeed two bake-houses, both absolutely identical. At the far end of the street was another, with a fourth fifty yards beyond. A fifth, again next door to a factory, and in this case an outdoor beer-house as well as a bakery, stood at the far end of the street where my father worked. Here too, within a distance of a few hundred yards, were three chapels; and this pattern of house, factory, bake-house and chapel, with here and there little front room sweet-shops, continued all over the town.

In photographs of these Midland streets taken in the first years of the century it is sometimes possible to see what the shoemakers of the day looked like. They were very often dressed in the sort of curly bowler now called Edwardian or in tile flat almost peakless cap that is again, like the bowler, popular today. Their jackets were longish, black and cut away, often with those capacious pockets called poachers' pockets, and no man ever wore anything on his feet but boots, never shoes, or anything but a muffler round his neck, except of course on holidays and Sundays. I can just remember these men, not only hurrying to work in the morning but hurrying during the course of the day from factory or back-yard work shop to the sewing and stitching shops, either carrying armfuls of boot uppers or wheeling them in big three-wheel basket trucks.

But what I really remember most vividly about these men are their aprons and mufflers. My father wore a muffler, the ends of which he crossed, folded over and tucked into his armpits exactly in the style of all other working men. He also wore an apron. This was of white cotton, with a white tape band to go over the head and two others to tie at the waist. It was more or less possible to tell the craft of a man from the degree of dirtiness on his apron. Clickers, the men who begin the whole process of shoe-making by cutting out from skins of leather the uppers, toe-caps, tongues, facings and so on, could keep their aprons clean for a long time, but finishers, who give the soles of shoes their final blacking and polishing, could never be clean, either as to aprons or hands, and my impression is that sometimes they wore wholly black aprons. On Sundays I myself wore a little apron, white and cut exactly like my father's, in order that I should avoid spilling gravy and pudding down my best blue serge waistcoat. I was not, of course, allowed to sit at table with my jacket on; nor did my father and nor indeed any other shoemaker or his son.

There were times when I took my father's tea to him at the factory in a blue enamel can with a cup balanced on the top. The plan of those old factories, all built just before the turn of the century, was very much the same: three storeys of brick, windows of thick opaque glass, heavy wooden front door, widish wooden staircase, and a little matchwood office on the first floor where clerks dealt with wages, kept books and made use of the wall

fixture telephone. I used to go to this dark, ugly, dreary, noisome, thunderous bedlam of industry with a sense of dread: not dread, I think, of its sheer drabness, its stench of leather and gas-light or its racket of presses and whining scream of machines, but a terrible dread at the half-conscious notion that one day I too might have to work in it. I did not then know that my father, the gentlest of men, had vowed before God that I never should work in it; nor did I know, until far beyond these earliest years of childhood, that he had begun work in that same bedlam at the age of ten, as a half-timer, and that for almost all of another fifty years he was to detest it.

The impression I chiefly gain from the recollection of those shoe-making men is not exactly one of coarseness; they lack the sheer belted belching muscle and guts of what used to be known as labouring men; they do not exhibit the beery-spitting swagger I remember of navvies, bricklayers or those wild-eyed drovers of cattle I sometimes used to see, drunk and rosy-eyed, on Midland market days. Their roughness is of rather a different order, and I find it difficult to describe. If I use the word rude, in the sense of uncouth, the impression will be a shade too strong. Nor are they loud; nor, in Rupert Brooke's words, excessively "black of mouth". Nor are they as forthright, or as blunt or as self-opinionated as Northern men. The impression I really get is of a dry, droll, unshaven independence and it is not at all an unlikeable quality.

This impression of unshaven men is a very real one and I think it springs largely from the fact that I saw these shoe-makers so often in barbers' shops. There were two barbers' shops to which I went in my childhood and both inflicted on me so considerable an amount of torture that even now, nearly half a century later, I still intensely dislike having my hair cut. It was my penance to have to go to them on Saturdays, an ill-favoured day as far as boys were concerned, since both saloons would be crammed from eight-o'clock onwards with crowds of shag-smoking, snuff-taking, stubble-faced working men, mufflered and capped, most of them waiting to be shaved. The system by which customers would be taken in strict rotation was something that worked very well with men but broke down instantly it came to the turn of a boy. In consequence I used to sit for three or four or even five hours in ever increasing boredom and despair, exhausting one by one the tattered pink copies of *Chips* and the tattered white copies of *Comic Cuts*, turning in eventual desperation to the bewildering pages of *Sporting Life* or, as I grew older, to the terrors of the *Police Gazette*. All the time, all about me, a lather boy would be ceaselessly brushing soap into three-day beards, and the barber himself — in one saloon a gossiping idiot of brainless nosiness, in the other a dapper little jockey-like man of sporty instinct — would be clipping, snipping and scraping away with scissors and cut-throat. The smell of shag, after two or three hours, had the power to move mountains, and in one corner there burned, like some semi-evil fire out of a picture of an opium den, the three-forked flames of a gas-geyser heating water. Many customers kept their own shaving mugs at the saloons and these stood about on shelves between advertisements for navy-cut, Wood-bines, plug, twist, the beloved shag and, most surprisingly, brands of cigars. And in odd corners there stood piles of umbrellas, that strange sideline of the provincial barbers' world, very much like piles of battered old rooks, brought in for repair.

I would say that the average shoemaker of those days, whether self-shaven or shop-shaven, had the razor on his face no more than twice or three times a week. My father shaved every day, but then my father was not an average shoemaker; whereas my grandfather, a man of an older, more rural, more home-spun generation, as I have described, shaved on Wednesdays and Saturdays unless some special mid-week evening took him out to political meetings or lectures, when he would again scrape off his beard and, in his own words, get himself titivated up. There were of course plenty of men who were great dandies in that generation — the moustache-waxers, the quiff-plasterers, the wearers of patent toe-caps — and these were exceptions to the two-shaves-a-week system, just as they were far removed from the habit of smoking shag in short nose-warming clays.

I do not wish to give the impression here that I am speaking of a generation composed entirely of uncouth louts: very much the contrary. The shoemakers of the Midlands have long been noted for their pride, political acumen, sturdy independence of mind and an ability to talk sense under conditions where others often signally fail. It is in fact from this same generation, so many of whom were to be wiped out in the holocaust of Somme and Passchendaele, that there sprang, to their abiding credit, an industrial arbitration system that has virtually kept the boot and shoe industry in England free from any kind of serious dispute or stoppage for over half a century. When dockers, miners, car-workers, railway men and bus drivers use what they so charmingly call the strike-weapon to back industrial grievance I become very proud of my shoemakers, the men who had the guts and sense to put an end to years of seemingly irremediable bitterness, hunger, lock-outs, strikes and sheer destitution by a system built on simple common-sense, honour and a rejection of acrimony. These were my shag-smokers, the unshaven ones. They lived very largely on kippers, bloaters, tea, beer, cheese, potatoes and plenty of good bread from the coal-ovened bake-houses; and the lordly inevitable roast-beef on Sundays. They were the ones who ran to work in fear of losing farthings, waking me every morning in my waking years.

A few years earlier, just too far back for me to remember, at a time when the old hand shoemaker and his world were passing for ever, the life of these towns was very much a man's domain. There was much brawling, fighting, drinking and sheer squabbling squalor. There also existed two kinds of animosity which townships no longer know: that between street and street, when gangs of louts brawled in small possessive warfare, and that between township and township, when men out of crude bravado rolled from one town to another, beating up rival gangs, rough-housing outside ever-open pubs and inventing strange labels of contempt for rival towns. "Hock-and-Dough" was a term still commonly used for Wellingborough, the market town with the public school on the Nene, when I was a child, the name deriving from some kind of poor man's dish of trotter and pastry said to be much favoured in that town but which the men of Rushden, the Evensford of my novels, held to be food beneath contempt. The men of Raunds, a rough little, tough little town with a rare church, had the jeer of Hair- and-Teeth thrown at them, and replied by calling the men of Irthlingborough Yow-Yows.

In that world, meanwhile, women drudged, slaved, pawned clothes, conceived, gave their children bread and scrat to eat and waited and wept. There was an extraordinary amount of tuberculosis in these valleys, both then and for many years later. Yellowish-blue faces, far gone in decline, peer at me through memory with haunting cadaverous thinness. The harrowing picture of Victorian industrial hunger has been too often painted for me to attempt it again, but there is no doubt that thousands of women of that masculine shoe-making world just before and perhaps even after my birth waited in desolation, Saturday after Saturday, for fools, braggarts, wasters and almost every other kind of husband to bring home the week's wages; and waited in vain. The Saturday drunken beat-up, when beer drowned every penny of a man's money, was as fixed a part of life as the Sunday morning parade to chapel and church; and women, dreading it, bled their hearts out.

If you care now to make a journey into this Midland shoe-making country I do not think that you will find, except for the factories themselves and the familiar brick street pattern, anything left of what I describe. A great number of the people of my native Evensford work, for example, in a factory designed by the late President of the Royal Academy, Sir Albert Richardson; and on Sundays enjoy music played in a band-stand, also designed by that eminent twentieth-century Georgian, standing in the park of the great house described in *Love for Lydia*. Men no longer wear aprons and mufflers or, I believe, run to work. Most of the old bake-houses are closed and I doubt very much if an old familiar cry, a great favourite of mine, the cry of the water-cress man, is ever heard on Sunday afternoons. Women please themselves what time they arrive in factory closing rooms, going in to work at nine or nine-thirty or two or two-thirty as they wish and leaving in the same way. Just before Christmas they festoon the workrooms with decorations and, unless my relatives in the boot and shoe towns misinform me, hold parties, complete with wine. Every man is a collar-and-tie man now and the girls and women, always so handsome and conscious of their clothes, are among the prettiest and best-dressed in England — the daughters and granddaughters, many of them, of those same women who bled their hearts out at Victorian street corners and in summer gleaned the surrounding fields for a winter's bread.

CHAPTER
FOUR

It has long been my impression that I went to school at the age of three, but my mother, now in her ninety-second year but happily possessed of all her faculties including a memory quite unimpaired, insists that I was four. In either case I remember the occasion vividly, having put on a gigantic tantrum (what my grandfather sometimes used to call "a mad" or "a paddy"), in my determination not to go. I was thwarted in this purpose, however, by the opportune arrival of my step-grandmother, a formidable lady who promptly seized me by the ear, lugged me away and deposited me unceremoniously on the steps of the council infant school, two streets away.

Whether I had inherited from my father an antipathy towards school it is difficult to say; but that I viewed the prospect of attending it with as much dread as going to prison there is absolutely no doubt. Like my father I did not at all relish the prospect of confinement; already, even at that age, I had tasted the free range of fields, hedgerows, woods and streams to such an extent that I was constantly thirsting to get back to them. I was also, I am sure, mostly frightened by the very thought of schoolteachers, whose habits of terror and whipping had already been fearfully etched on my mind by older children only too keen to exaggerate their experience of school-going and its pain.

The immediate district served by this, my first school, was almost wholly working class. It is true that on the very eastern edge of the town, where open country began, there were incongruously a few affluent properties, fairly large houses set in well timbered grounds where teacups tinkled on lawns on summer afternoons and the clock of croquet balls might sometimes be heard, but much in the surrounding streets was near sordid, an adjective not inapplicable to some of my early class mates. "They make me sit next to a boy who stinks," I one day informed my mother and to this day the peculiar acrid stench of the unwashed lingers in my nostrils. Not only were many unwashed indeed — I suppose there was not more than one bathroom to a thousand houses in those days — but sometimes as I trailed to school a door in a row of terrace houses would open to give a swift and revolting picture of unmitigated squalor, of filthy rags spread about a carpetless floor, a gas stove ghastly with grease, a packing case serving as a chair and as likely as not a chamber pot, unwashed too, on prominent display on a broken chair. Small wonder that many of the children from these homes were in a constant state of itch and scratch, so that it needed all my father's vigilance and industry with soap and tooth-comb to keep me, as he would say, free of livestock.

But not all were unwashed. I still have in my possession a faded photograph of my class in the year, probably, of 1910, and a highly interesting social document it is. Three significant things are at once to be noted about it: all the little girls are wearing rather long flouncy pinafores; nine-tenths of the boys are wearing large, almost flamboyant white lace collars over their jackets, sometimes so big as to stretch to the tips of their shoulders; the other tenth are, however, dressed in plain dark blue jerseys, buttoning at the neck. These jerseys are what would now be called status symbols. The boys wearing them are sons of fathers higher up the social ladder or, as the shoemakers themselves used to put it so aptly, of men who are "notch above a tapper". I am one of them.

My brain is a quick and receptive one and I learned to read at an early age. The influence of my father is again apparent here; being able to read is one thing, having something to read is another. Where so many fathers of the unwashed wasted their pitiful substance on booze and betting my father was putting much of his into his piano, music and books. The end of the nineteenth century was notable for a considerable revolution in the world of popular newspapers and magazines, a revolution largely instigated in Fleet Street by the Harmsworth brothers, and to several of these magazines my father became an avid subscriber. *The Strand*, *The Harmsworth*, *The Windsor* and a rather preachy affair called *Young England* were among them and these he would subsequently have bound up into fat, half leather volumes.

The result of all this was that at quite an early age I began to have access to the work of Conan Doyle, Kipling, Barrie and a considerable number of other late

Victorian and Edwardian writers. I revelled in Holmes and *The Speckled Band*, smelled the putrefying rats in *Stalky & Co* and even swallowed the Scottish treacle of Barrie, never my favourite writer, and the fine doings of Captain Kettle. As my father's library grew it also revealed most curious divisions of taste: on the one hand there were tomes of insufferable solemnity on subjects divine and theological, on the other hand were works by William le Queux, E. Phillips Oppenheim, Conan Doyle, Edgar Wallace and a now rather forgotten though excellent French writer of detective stories, Gaboriau, creator of what I suppose was a sort of French Holmes, *Arsène Lupin*.

Like Graham Greene, I am sure that as I devoured these writers I unconsciously assimilated something of their methods — by which I mean the way all of them had no time for wasting words but had to make their points economically and incisively, rejecting all highly descriptive padding: an assimilation which, though unconscious at the time, as I say, was later to emerge as a guiding principle when I myself began to handle the short story. Even now I can remember expressing sharp impatience if a story went on too long, an impatience that has probably led to my disposition to stop stories short, leaving the reader in a state of speculative suspense and wondering guesswork, rather than take him on to a well-ordered and boring end.

In all these things I was fully engrossed by the age of 9 or 10; but some time before this, I suppose when I was 7 or 8, an event of some scholastic significance occurred. I suddenly found myself removed from the main body of my class, given a separate and special desk of my own and there set down to pursue work much in advance of that done by other pupils. A rapid climb followed and soon I was soaring away to the top of the main school, a circumstance that in no way prevented my joining in the rough-and-tumble of playground, football field or the long-since lost arena of street games. I have never, thank God, been in danger of becoming a male blue stocking.

The world of street games is not only far distant; it has slipped away for ever. The author of *South Wind*, Norman Douglas, writing some years before my time, published what is now a rare book, *London Street Games*, in which he recorded something like a thousand games. Though we played nothing like this formidable and fascinating number we nevertheless played a great many and were never short of a game for all seasons. Not the least curious feature of these games was the intensely guarded and parochial conditions under which they were played. Like jungle cocks jealously defending their territories or cock robins their patch of garden, each street rigorously repelled and rejected all others except perhaps its very nearest neighbour. Thus the children of Grove Street, in which my parents' house faced the gas-lights of the pork-butcher's shop and the two bake-houses, never dreamed of consorting with Crabb Street, from which we might have been removed by a thousand miles, even though we were not more than two hundred yards apart.

The ritual of street games went on freely and un-hampered, summer and winter, except in the very severest weather. There was no danger. A bicycle or two, a baker's cart trundling home with its golden candles trembling in the lamps, a late horse-drawn dray delivering a load of belly leather or packing cases to a factory before going back to the railway yards: these were about the only hazards we might expect to disturb us. The street was not only ours; we were expected, and ordered, to play there.

So, fortified in my case by hot tea, hot toast spread with home-made lard and salt — and how very good it was — we all went out, on early winter evenings, to the gas-lit street stage. I remember the winter evenings more vividly, I suppose, than the summer ones simply because of the gas-light: the one big street light round which we played

Sally go Round the Moon
Sally go Round the Stars
Sally go Round the Chimney Pot
On a Sunday afternoon

and the lights of the three shops.

Almost always, I think, we first gathered round the window of one of the bakers' shops to sort out preliminaries for play. Certain preliminaries had always to be gone through, among them the picking of teams, and also "who was going to start it". We always did this by rhymes. Thus, as we gathered in a circle, one of us went round, pointing to each in turn, reciting:

47

Paddy on the railway, picking up stones,
Down came the engine and broke Paddy's bones.
Well, said Paddy, that isn't fair.
Well, said the engine, I don't care.
O — U — T spells
"Out Goes She"

or we varied it thus:

Ink, Pink
I think
There is
A stink
And it comes from
YOU!
O — U — T spells
"Out Goes She"

After this the teams divided up, one going to the far
side of the street, the other remaining by the shop
window, so to speak on home ground. The main games
in this category, in all probability having origins going
back for centuries, were *I Apprentice My Son*, *I Spy*,
Three Old Men Come Workhouse and *What's Your
Trade?* though the last two may well have been slightly
different versions of the same thing. Norman Douglas, I
think, records all these as London games. There were
also various versions of Tick or Tag, one with the odd
name of *Chibby* (or *Chivy*) *up the Rat's Hole*, probably
the same game as Norman Douglas' *Chivy Chase*,
another *Cockerels*, which he doesn't mention. In due

season we played *Whip-and-Top*, *Hop Scotch* and *Marbles* — incredible now to think we played marbles across the full width of the street, from gutter to gutter, quite unhampered. There were also various versions of *Hide-and-Seek*, one with the curious name of *Hi-Acky* or perhaps *Hi-Yacky*, a name I thought for many years to be no more than a piece of meaningless local childhood slang, until I discovered it to be a corruption of the Latin *Hic Jacet* (*Here lies*) — in other words the call you make when hidden, inviting others to come and find you.

Girls of course played some games which most boys considered to be cissy: hop-scotch, buttons (you had a collection of old buttons which you picked up one by one from the pavement by wetting your thumb, pressing hard and hoping that the buttons would stick), skipping, and various ball games. There was also jackstones or five-stones, at which girls were at least as good as boys if not better (a certain girl I met much later was an absolute dabster at this and still isn't by any means a novice) but girls as far as I remember were never invited to play with us at cat-and-stick. For this you needed a stout stick and a second shortish stick, "the cat", sharpened at both ends. You could draw a chalk ring on the pavement as your playing arena, but we mostly preferred to play on man-hole covers. The loser of the toss first stood with eyes shut, feet at ten-past-ten on the perimeter of the manhole cover and head well back, with the "cat" balanced on his forehead. "The cat" was then allowed to roll off his forehead, down his nose and into the ring below. According to how the cat fell, whether in the ring, out of it or touching the perimeter, so you were allowed a certain number of strikes with the stick. The technique was to strike the cat smartly at the sharpened end so that it leapt in the air. As it leapt you hit it. If you were lucky enough to have three strikes you could end up by hitting it as much as thirty yards. Whatever length it was you had to "offer it up", so to speak, to your opponent. Thus you guessed ten, or twenty or thirty yards and your opponent then either gave you the number or offered to "measure you out". This he did by striding out the yards from manhole cover to "cat". If he "measured you out" it was then his turn, since his gamble had failed. Cat-and-stick I always loved; it was a great game for hand, leg and eye.

Of *Cat-and-Stick* I can find no mention in Douglas' *London Street Games*, a book that, incidentally, was rejected by a number of publishers before it finally appeared in the middle of the First World War, when its "flurried accumulation" and apparently "casual methods" irritated some critics and its contents may well have appeared to the general public as being of slight importance in comparison with the games being played in the company of blood, lice, rats, mud, shell-holes and other barbarous futilities on the fields of Flanders. But one critic at least had a remark of sage and indeed prophetic importance to say of it and after fifty years of social standardization and reform its truth seems to have an even sharper significance: "one marvels at the stupidity of the social reformer who desires to close to the children the world of adventure, to take from them their birthright of the streets, and coop them up in well-regulated and uninspiring play-grounds where, under the supervision of teachers, their imagination will decline, their originality wither." To this Douglas himself added: "The standardization of youth proceeds relentlessly; it is part of what Richard Aldington calls the insane process of making great groups happy by destroying the personal happiness of every individual in that group; it is one of the many steps in the direction of that termite-ideal towards which we are trending."

How many of these street games are still played? was Douglas' final question, and if the question even then had about it a note of despair it is one of utter futility today. The termites have taken over. In place of *Cat-and-Stick* youth plays at shoplifting; instead of the hurry-burly of *Mop-stick*, an hilarious version of *Leap-frog* which was my favourite of all street games, it stages protesting marches of babble and rabble against this and that; in the place of *Chibby Up the Rat's Hole* it prefers to crawl up the devious rats' holes of drugs; in its new-found affluence it no longer kicks a football made of newspaper tied with string about streets and alleys but sings ballads licentious and malodorous at supposedly first-class matches; it prefers violence to marbles; it would rather wreck trains, public conveniences and shop-windows than run off its energies at *Stag* and *Cockerels*. Termites, after all, can only be expected to behave like termites in a termite-world.

Searching for possible origins for these many street games Douglas treated with scorn the theorising notion of his fictitious Aunt Eliza that *London Bridge is Broken Down* went "back to bloodthirsty rites of foundation-sacrifice", that *Fie Sally, Cry Sally* originated in early water-worship and that *Here We Come Gathering Nuts in May* was "a relic of marriage by capture". More and more I fear that Douglas' scorn was misplaced. He had evidently forgotten that one form of water-worship, still calculated to have circus audiences rolling in the aisles, is one of the oldest pantomimic jokes in the world; that in the world of entertainment the fascination of "Marriage by Capture" never palls; and that blood, whether on the sacrificial altars of a more ancient world, the arenas of bull-fighting and fox-hunting, or in the tribal warfare of football fields, still exercises and satisfies a remorseless universal taste.

We are all playing games, adults perhaps even more than children, and most of them are far far older than those Douglas collected so assiduously from London's streets or that I played on winter evenings under the long since departed gas-light of the baker's shop.

CHAPTER
FIVE

That the golden days with my grandfather must have been interspersed with dark and dismal ones I have no doubt; but I find it hard to recall them. The days in the hayfield were always hot, those in the harvest-field even hotter. Always the air in June seems to have been clotted with the intoxication of mown grass, of may-blossom, of moon-daisies dying along the paling swathes. In August the great bearded, or horned wheat — surely another of my grandfather's mistakes — undoubtedly stood higher than a man, dark brown and rough indeed like a beard, the straw tough as reed and as difficult to mow, the sheaves correspondingly prodigious of weight. The heavy clay land dried out to concrete, splitting under the heat into fissures wide enough to swallow the foot of a man, let alone of a boy. All, it must be remembered, was done by hand. Try as I would, and try though my grandfather did to teach me, I was never really able to make bonds for the great bearded sheaves. The bonds always slipped and broke; the sheaves collapsed as I manfully tried to bear them to the stooks, the beards and docks and drying thistles stabbing into my small bare arms.

Just before half past twelve we always started to look

down the road for the little figure of my grandmother, bringing up the dinner baskets. She never failed to appear, nipping quickly along. Back in Victorian days my grandfather had gone over the Bedfordshire border, to the tiny village of Souldrop, on the edge of the valley of the Ouse, to court his bride. No one was ever better named than Priscilla Bird. She looked indeed for ever like a bird: perhaps most aptly a wren, tiny, quick, bright-eyed, sharp, indefatigable. After the fashion of her day she went out, as a young girl, to service, one result of which was that she cooked superbly, another that her household was always scrupulously, miraculously clean. Whenever I remember her I smell baking bread, roasting beef, soap-suds, starch, bees-wax and hot irons. Scarcely possible though it is to believe, she had a sister, Matilda, who kept *The Chequers Inn* over the Bedfordshire border at the village of Yelden, (well-known to many an American service man) who was even cleaner. Her pub tables were scrubbed until they looked like scoured stone; her bar gleamed like an altar.

Our dinner in the harvest-field was always hot; none of your makeshift lumps of dough with onions stuffed into them: a dish known as a Bedfordshire Clanger; no lumps of cold bacon and bread, no plain bread-and-cheese, no sandwiches. In one basket would repose a steak-and-kidney pie, perhaps a rabbit pie, or a beef pudding, together with basins of new potatoes, carrots, peas or beans: all wrapped in clean white napkins. In the other there would be, perhaps, an apple pie or, what I myself loved best of all, a pie of a small yellow local plum of extraordinarily good flavour and rather squarish in shape and touched with a faint blush of crimson, very like an apricot.

To eat all this we sat, on very hot days, in the shade of a vast ash-tree, or if the weather were a little cooler, in the shelter of a wheat stook. All about us the deep summer silence spread in a vast hush broken only, though really accentuated, by the whirr of grasshoppers and occasionally, from down the hedgerows, the crooning song of yellow hammers, deepening the silence too with their endless "little bit of bread-and-cheese". "Pass the pepper and walt, boy," my grandfather would say and eventually, replete, would fall into a doze, at which signal I crept away along the hedgerow to look for the first dew-berries, the sweet-sharp taste of which still bursts on my tongue as the true juice of full summer.

Always indefatigable, my grandmother was back at half past four, this time with one basket and a big blue can of tea. Now perhaps we sat in the stack-yard, under a haystack, out of the glare of the western sun. My grandmother always baked her own bread, which I called "mucky bread" because of its dark brown shade. My grandfather always ate this bread with its butter side down, insisting that only in this way could you really taste bread-and-butter. With it we ate dark red plum or damson jam and afterwards there was perhaps dough-cake, a bread with currants and sultanas in it, and another great favourite of mine, caraway cake, which my grandmother baked exquisitely. All about us, as we ate, sat a large bevy of cats and kittens, waiting for a saucer of tea and scraps of bread-and-butter, while in the

pig-sties the pigs worked up their own appetite, beginning to scream hungrily on the hot afternoon.

After tea my grandmother left us and soon a man with the redoubtable name of Smack arrived. Shoemaker by day, he turned into pure peasant countryman by evening, beery, cunning, masterly with whet-stone and scythe. For so small a man he had a tireless and astonishing strength. The tall powerful stalks of horned wheat fell before his scythe-blade with a great crisp, crushing sound, the fallen swathes beautifully and perfectly laid, no stalk out of place. Sometimes a hare or a leveret would start up out of the corn and all tools were downed as we set off on the hunt, which more often than not was fruitless, and occasionally the scythe-blade would be dramatically stilled and poised in air and a whisper from Smack would tell us that he had stopped short, just in time, of a late nest of partridge eggs.

In those days, before the lavish use of weed-killers, which have now done so much to ravage the wild-life of the English countryside, birds, butterflies and flowers alike, the cornfield was flowery from end to end. Tiny red periwinkles, pink convolvulus, occasional corn-cockles, cinquefoil, camomile, blue cornflowers and endless scarlet poppies spread themselves everywhere. As the scythe bared the wheat down to stubble, the poppies, cornflowers and corn-cockles all laid low, a sort of creeping garden of all the prostrate, tiny things remained. They are indeed tiny things to remember for ever but they persist in my mind, with both joy and affection, long after greater things have faded. There also persists, in utter contrast, the sight of the great lines of stooks, at last set up like tents ready for camping in the evening sun. I sometimes crept into these tents, to be embalmed by that eternal, warm, friendly fragrance that only straw can give; and it was this fragrance, eternal indeed and as old as civilised man and his earth, that lingered with me as I went home at last in the deepening summer twilight, often so tired that I had to be carried, my face and hands and arms and legs scratched by stubble, bitten by harvest-bugs and as mucky in colour as my grandmother's "mucky bread".

Beyond Souldrop, in the larger village of Sharnbrook, my grandmother had another sister, Mary Ann. Here the wide pastoral view of the Ouse Valley opens up to its full breadth and beauty: the river itself white with water-lilies in summer, the woods rich in spring with primrose and oxlip, the pastures soft and luscious. If the villages today are no longer locked in the dreaminess I knew more than half a century ago their velvety, v-stitched, dreamy names remain: Turvey, Stevington, Odell, Felmersham, Lavendon, Newton Blossomville.

My grandmother's sister, also an excellent cook, especially as I remember it of potatoes, which she always served with a particularly delicious butter sauce, lived a short distance outside the village of Sharnbrook, in a tiny thatched cottage, at the top of a rough stony track, on the edge of a wood. This wood remains, for me, a paradise: crowded in spring with violets, both purple and white, primroses, anemones and later bluebells and pink campion. In high summer its fringes were red with wild strawberries. In June, after the gold of cowslips had faded, the fields on all sides were white with moon daisies and deeply fragrant with red clover. Not far away the main railway line from London to the North runs up the long escarpment of the river valley and it is still the sound of the great double engined steam expresses rushing magnificently past, shattering the woodland silence with a thousand echoes, that remains as vividly with me as the sight and sound of flowers and the song of thrush, blackbird and nightingale.

Even more vividly remains the picture of cottage and garden. The little low-ceilinged rooms are for ever steeped in the smell of wood smoke; from the walls look down faded sepia portraits of Victorian relatives dressed in Sunday best; dried bulrushes, feathery brushes of pampas grass and the silvery coinage of dried honesty seed decorate the mantelpiece with its drapery of claret velvet. Outside the door, always open in summer, there grew a bush of that old enchantress of a rose, *Maiden's Blush*, surrounded by white Madonna lilies, double white pinks, larkspur, poppies, marigolds and cottage favourites of that sort. In the longish stretch of garden extending to the very edge of the wood there were gooseberry trees bearing fruit of such size that they might well have been inflated, like balloons, together with white and red currants and, unless my memory tricks me, a golden yellow raspberry of choicest flavour. Rows of peas, beans, sweet-peas rose from a soil black as only soil long cultivated and long enriched can be. Most vivid of all a scarlet Turk's Cap lily flaunted a kingly head above the crowd of common cottage subjects, like a strange aristocrat from another world.

This scarlet lily is the key that unlocks the world of a

certain Joseph Betts, husband of my grandmother's sister. Born in the Hungry Forties, reprobate, rapscallion, crafty as a monkey, liar, gardener of much cunning, drinker of infinite capacity, afflicted with one blood-shot eye that gave him a look of devilish fascination, he is the original of My Uncle Silas, the character whose alcoholic and womanising adventures I was to chronicle in a series of stories some twenty-five years later. Sitting propped by the kitchen door in corduroy trousers and a thick old bread-cloth waistcoat, he was, to a small boy, a figure both compelling and fearsome. An aura of positively Satanic secrecy surrounded his prowess in raising gooseberries big as golf balls, potatoes unmatched for earliness and flavour, peas of unrivalled succulence and most of all the presence of the Turk's Cap lily. As he supped at glasses of home-brewed cowslip and elderberry wine — in spring the kitchen floor would often be yellow with sheets of drying cowslips — I listened to him with ears cocked and eyes utterly hypnotised. Already he then seemed to me to be venerable, almost patriarchal, a figure from a past even more remote than Hardy's early novels. He was in fact still to ripen to an even greater age, living into his nineties, for ever growing more crafty, devilish and fearsome, so much so that one day when I much later took my future wife to meet him for the first time she was as near terrified, poor girl, as if I had presented Old Nick himself.

From those golden days at the little cottage by the woodside there stands out one gilded with special splendour: a summer day when my mother, my grandmother, my aunt, my sister and myself arrived there for the wedding of Joe Betts' only son. By the generosity of the local squire a big white marquee had been put up in the little paddock; inside it long trestle tables were filled with cold meats and sandwiches and salads and cakes and beer and wine. Already by the time we arrived Joe was as merry as a boozy cricket; by afternoon he was rollicking; by evening he was prancing with the ladies; by dusk he was drunkenly bawling *We won't go home till morning! — let 'em all come!*, the leading jester on an uproarious summer stage. Such was the sharpness of the impression it all made on me that though it was a near quarter of a century before I put it down in a story called *The Wedding* the words practically wrote themselves.

Joe too belongs to a vanished world. His little thatched cottage, so a correspondent writes to tell me, has been pulled down. The world of television, jets and space craft dazzles our generation with new if sometimes near useless wonders, but for myself I would cheerfully exchange it all for that blood-shot eye, the smell of woodsmoke, the scent of bluebells, cowslips, primroses and the Maiden's Blush, the Turk's Cap lily and the voices of nightingales.

CHAPTER
SIX

My father was a diligent early riser. Indeed he always conveyed the impression that there was something slightly immoral about remaining in bed after seven o'clock. On Sundays it is true that he relaxed a little, though even then if you arrived a minute or two late for eight o'clock breakfast you were more than likely to get a look of some severity and a cryptic and admonishing "You're last!" that might have been in itself a foretaste of the stern Sabbath pattern of the day to come.

A small sweetener, however, brightened the early morning before Sunday really claimed us body and soul. On the piano stood two white china swans. Miraculously, overnight, they had always laid eggs in the shape of little packets of chocolates wrapped in blue, green, scarlet and silver tinfoil and tied with narrow coloured ribbons, and I never failed to search for and discover them with a sensation of excitement, astonishment and joy.

At a quarter to nine Sunday began. Dressed in my best blue serge with a big white Eton collar, I made my way to Sunday school. The old chapel, now the school, was barely two streets away. My route to it took me by the factory next door, then past the Band Club, where much blowing and practising on silver wind instruments continually enlivened the summer evening air, past another factory and my father's factory next door, past a little farm where I often went to fetch a penny can of milk, and finally past a Baptist chapel and yet another factory.

If I was not oppressed by quite the same feeling of dread with which I went so long to day school I was nevertheless always haunted on Sundays by a secret sensation of impending imprisonment. Rain, fog, frost, hail, snow: there was never the remotest chance of escaping. With me I took a sort of passport, a star-card, which I duly presented at the Sunday school door to have stamped with a violet star as proof of my punctual attendance. Once inside I was captured by an air that somehow yet remains with me as dusty musty, over-sanctified. I am unfamiliar with what contemporary Methodism now produces in the way of its more dedicated adherents, but fifty years ago it was still dominated by stern and tyrannical believers who upheld the piety of silence, were convinced that even whispering among boys was a sin and had no compunction about boxing the ears of the recalcitrant with bible or hymn book as penalty for the minutest misdemeanour. Often the sternest of these mentors were men converted from the wickedness and evils of looser living, more often than not drink, and were now purified and on the narrow path of righteousness. Later, in chapel, inspired by some divine inner fervour, they would sometimes leap suddenly to their feet or drop down on bended knees and cry aloud to Heaven in the blessed name of the Lord, as if having seen a vision. "Praise Him!" they would shout, "Bless His name! Glory be and grant us mercy!"

No doubt on the principle that "the devil finds work for idle hands to do" we were kept in close confinement at Sunday school for close on two hours, singing hymns, locked in prayer, listening to windy homilies, reading biblical chapter and verse. The pews were hard, the slow dragging minutes intolerable. This, however, was merely the beginning of our sanctified day. At a quarter to eleven we were shepherded into chapel, there to undergo a repeat adult performance of what we had already suffered. If anything the homilies were even windier, the pews harder, the silences longer and harder to bear. Methodism decrees that its preachers shall move on a three year circuit, so that at intervals a new face appeared in the pulpit. Sometimes we were harangued by humourless, impassioned Welshmen. Occasionally there appeared a local preacher, as often as not a half-literate from some remote village, burdened with strong country accent, unravelling a long tangled skein of biblical rhetoric (*"Now what did our good Lord mean by them there words?"* etc.) droning on and on until not only children became restless but even adults started fidgeting with watches, and hungry bellies rattled.

At last came the blessed relief of the anthem, the taking of the collection and then the last hymn. Sure enough it would have an intolerable number of verses, not one to be cut. Then all eyes closed for the final benediction. As often as not that too would be long drawn-out, developing sometimes into yet another homily. By this time it might well be half past twelve, the hour at which everybody except the beer-swillers at clubs and pubs ate their midday dinner. The sensation of being released into fresh open air was unbelievably sweet. Hungry, my bottom aching, I hurried home to meet a procession peculiar to the times: that of men hurrying from bake-houses, bearing Sunday dinners of roast meat and Yorkshire pudding, sizzling in baking tins and covered with cloths to keep them hot. After the nightly bread-baking, with the fires damped down, the big coal ovens were perfect for cooking pudding and meat: charge, a penny.

At home, as I have already said, I took off my Sunday jacket and put on my little white apron before sitting down to eat. Always, in the true Midland tradition, we ate pudding first and meat afterwards, a practice my father insistently continued all through his life. (My grandfather maintained that in his day the pudding was eaten from the underside of the plate, after which the plate was turned right side up for the meat.) No drink, not even a glass of water, was allowed throughout the meal ("It'll only blow you up," I was always told), but after dinner I was allowed the luxury of a bar or two of the chocolates the white swans had laid, before — yes, it isn't hard to guess — going yet again to Sunday school.

The devil, I fear, had a poor time of it on those Midland Sundays. For a third time we were imprisoned, this time for a mere hour, but often, as if this were still not enough, we were ushered yet again to chapel, to listen perhaps to a diatribe by some missionary home from China or to what was called a "sacred concert" or an oratorio. Even then there loomed before us the prospect of a fifth term, that of evening chapel at six, though I must here be honest and admit that, in my early childhood at any rate, we were granted release from this either to visit my grandfather and his pigs or to walk tranquilly across footpaths in summer fields. Yet with the same honesty I must record that there often imposed itself upon us yet a sixth term, that of a late prayer meeting, where Methodist fervours, far from dwindling after the long day's devotions, gathered new life, so that the converted visionaries were once again inspired to leap to their feet, blessing and praising the Lord's Holy name and thanking Him for providential deliverance from the evil of their ways.

Truly the Methodists were iron shepherds to their sheep; yet if the Sundays of my childhood seem over-disciplined they compare quite favourably with those of my mother, who had to rise at a quarter to six every Sunday in order to attend a first service at half past and then had yet another session thrown in at five o'clock in the afternoon — little relaxation for a girl of eleven already working half-time.

CHAPTER
SEVEN

There is a Divinity which shapes our ends, rough-hew them how we will. Shakespeare's words, as so often, vividly and succinctly enshrine truths which lesser men merely grope to discover. In the year 1916, rough-hewn though my young life might perhaps have been until that time, the first but by no means the last of several divinity-shapings imposed itself upon me.

But it is first necessary to go back a couple of years: to the Easter of 1914. In the spring of that year two events of importance occurred. First, my step-grandmother decided to join my paternal grandfather in Australia, to which he had emigrated some time before, largely on the grounds of poor health. A story arising from this does much to demonstrate that though my grandfather may have been something of a philanderer — which is perhaps putting it mildly — he was by no means lacking in shrewdness. It would appear that some time before these events he had become involved in some sort of business deal with a man who eventually either went bankrupt or welshed on him. As to the details I have never been clear, but when the resulting mess came to be sifted and straightened out the solicitors dealing with the affair offered my grandfather a modest lump sum out of the wreckage or, if he preferred it, two pounds a week for life, a not inconsiderable sum in the early years of the century. There seems little doubt that in making this attractive offer they were not uninfluenced by the state of my grandfather's health, no doubt reasoning that two pounds a week was the more advantageous settlement from their point of view. Wisely my grandfather accepted it and went on receiving the two pounds a week for the rest of his life, or for a good thirty-five years or more.

The first immediate result of my step-grandmother's decision to emigrate was that the villa my grandfather had built for himself in 1900 had become available for my father, profiting now from his early years of thrift and prudence, to buy. One of my grandfather's favourite winter resorts had been Menton, the name by which the villa was duly called. It is a house very typical of a time when boot manufacturers were making money fast and providing themselves with a higher status and new degrees of comfort: solid red brick with stone facings, quite spacious dining-room and drawing-room and the almost unbelievable luxury of a bathroom. In his determination to give the house a still further touch of class my grandfather had even called in Italian workmen to lay floors of multi-coloured mosaic in hall-way and passages. No doubt he had been impressed by all this in Italy and Menton but had neglected to question the entire unsuitability of cold mosaic floors for the English climate. In winter both hall-way and passages were consequently more frigid than a tomb.

With the house, set in a street that incredibly had no

factory, no bake-house, no club, pub or chapel, though Bunyan's old meeting-house still stood and in fact still stands, just round the corner, went a reasonably spacious walled garden, complete with greenhouse and summer-house. This my father had, with his usual aptitude for making good use of his hands, already planted up with fruit trees, on his father's behalf, some ten years before. Now the walls were furnished with maturing Doyenne du Comice and Williams Bon Chrétien pears, together with Victoria plums yielding fruit of incomparable size and succulence. There were many apple trees, most of them of Victorian and Edwardian varieties no longer grown or seen, though none the worse for that, and there was a positive forest of gooseberries, black, white and red currants and raspberry canes. To move into such a house and garden after the very modest terrace we had occupied, penned in on one side by the walls of a factory, from which came the eternal whine of machines and the thunder of presses, was a tremendous leap up the social ladder and I have no doubt that I, at the age of nine, was probably more than a little snobbish about it all. But equally there is no doubt that its acquisition reflects the very greatest credit on my father, whose own childhood years of misfortune, penury, truancy and unhappiness were not so very far behind him.

On the eve of Good Friday that year, 1914, my father and mother departed for London to say farewell and wish *Bon Voyage* to my step-grandmother at Tilbury Docks, leaving me behind. Quite why I didn't go to stay as usual with my other grandfather I cannot now remember, but what I do remember, and that most vividly, was that someone or other had come up with the inspired suggestion that I should briefly set up in business on Good Friday, for the purpose of selling Hot-Cross buns. For some days beforehand I accordingly went about calling on neighbours with my little order book, recording orders for a dozen buns here, two dozen there and so on. On the eve of Good Friday I could hardly sleep for excitement. Next morning I must have been up at six o'clock and across the road, in the bake-house, complete with large clothes basket and clean white cloth, by half past, ready to pick up my first load of fresh warm buns.

It is very natural that I should cherish a great fondness for that old bake-house. I suppose I was in there, for some purpose or other, to fetch bread or flour or yeast or just to stare, almost every day. There was always a great heavenly embalming warmth about it, together with the even heavenlier fragrance of new-baked bread. The big low bread ovens, hung about with wooden peels for sliding dough in and loaves out, were dark and fascinating caverns. The baker, a thin, rather ill-looking, cadaverous man, always appeared to be saturated with ghostlike clouds of whiteness. In the little yard outside the bakery his horse and baker's cart were stabled. A pile of soddened dung always steamed on the air, the ammoniac sting of it powerful enough to kill even the aroma of baking. On winter nights a weary looking horse and an even wearier-looking baker came home at walking pace, journeyings done, the golden candle flames in the cart-lamps flabbily flickering in the dark air.

Good Friday, as far back as I can remember, has

always been the most dismal, the most inaptly named day of the year. Only a few weeks ago, as I write this, I was in Switzerland on Good Friday; it was bitterly cold and raining; there was much fresh snow on the mountains. At my hotel the young lady receptionist hugged her shoulders and said: "Always, always it is the same. Always on Good Friday." So indeed it would appear to be: a day that seems always to be cursed with rain and cold and darkness at noon.

But at least one Good Friday in my life, that of 1914, is filled with light. My impression is that I was given the traditional Baker's dozen when I collected my buns, so that I was able to make a little extra profit. Another impression is that I was so keen and eager to get my orders delivered that I was too early for many customers, quite half of whom were not up when I first called, so that I was forced to call again, often to be greeted by sleepy-eyed, disgruntled ladies in curling pins. It was a tradition in those days — I doubt very greatly if it persists today — that the buns should be delivered hot and to that end I went back to the bake-house several times for fresh hot supplies, always keeping them carefully covered with the clean white cloth. The weather too was true to its tradition, the early morning typically dismal and chill as I remember, but for once I never really felt it. My heart was as warm with excitement as the buns.

When war broke out in August of that year, although I was only nine, I was acutely conscious of a dark and enshrouding shadow. At least one part of the world that was about to be destroyed and to vanish for ever still seems to me like a delicate, decorated meringue. It was my parents' custom to take us, every August, to the seaside. For one week only, since these were the days long before paid holidays, when one week was the statutory holiday for the average worker, we moved into a world of sea and sunlight, sand and promenades, gentlemen in blazers and boaters, fishermen and jolly rowing in *The Skylark*, ladies in flowered hats and hobble skirts, military bands playing light music on piers and in bandstands, and the elegance of Sunday morning church parades.

When you live absolutely in the centre of a country, as we did in Northamptonshire, the sight of the sea on a shining summer's day can only be likened to the sudden sight of the Promised Land. It is yet another example of blessed escape from imprisonment. Several times we went north to Scarborough and pleasant though the memories of that agreeable watering place still are it is really to the south country that I find the mind's eye turning over and over again with greater pleasure. Indeed it is not too much to say that when the train rushed out of the first tunnel through the chalk of the North Downs, into the wide pastoral of Kent and Sussex, I never failed to get a strong impression that somehow this was my second home, this rich and varied cornucopia of fruit and corn and pasture and hops, of woodland and hills and oast-houses, that makes the Midland plain of grass and elm look about as appetising as a slice of stale bread. It was to be nearly another twenty years before the desire to live there became a fully conscious one but when at last it did come and was amply fulfilled the sense of escape from imprisonment was as powerful as ever.

Brighton, Hastings, St Leonards, Worthing, Eastbourne we went to stay in all of them in turn and we were at a modest little boarding establishment at Eastbourne when war broke out. It is odd how the recollection of little things over and over again creates the most powerful impression: the smell of sea, of seaweed drying in the sun, of plaice being fried for breakfast, or horse dung and the whiff of vinegar from whelk-stalls. The memory of sea-side Sundays is strong and brilliant too. Here again, even on holiday, the hand of Methodism still took its stern grip on us. Even to set foot on the beach on the Sabbath Day was forbidden. Buckets and spades and balls and bathing drawers were put away as if they were devices of the devil. Others might trip down the steps of horse-drawn bathing cabins to disport themselves in the Sunday sea, but not us. Donkey rides, games, running, ice-creams, pop: all were taboo. Circumspectly we strolled along the promenade at a pace unhurried and dignified, my father in straw boater and white buck-skin boots, my mother in mutton-leg sleeves and with the then fashionable band of black velvet round her neck. Like a scene from Monet or Renoir, the elegant church parade of straw hats, parasols and long sweeping ladies' skirts flowed towards and past us, while in the road the few blessed rich rode past in open Darracqs and Daimlers, Renaults and Rolls Royces with almost the grandeur of parading royalty, scornfully overtaking horse drawn landaus and an occasional sight-seeing brake or wagonette. Perhaps memory cheats a

74

little, perhaps it doesn't; perhaps the scene wasn't quite all elegance, all charm, all grace, all opulence, as the rose spectacles of fifty years appear to depict it, but one thing is quite certain: it was all about to be utterly shattered, for ever destroyed.

Before the sense of destruction made itself fully felt — even a child couldn't escape the eventual insufferable gloom of the holocaust that every morning was reflected in the long columns of the dead, wounded and missing that darkened every newspaper and still more intimately in the little mourning shrines set up in every street with their own lists of agonies and pitiful jam jars of flowers — I went through a period of martial excitement. War suddenly became glorified — or perhaps it would be truer to say that it merely became glamourised.

I am not now absolutely sure how long the war had been in progress when an advance party of billeting officers suddenly descended on the town, chalking what seemed to me to be meaningless sets of numbers and figures on the walls of houses. Soon the town was full of the sound of marching feet, the bang and blare of army bands and the voices of babbling Welshmen. The Royal Welch Fusiliers, disporting their famous black flash behind the tunic collar and their equally famous goat mascot at the head of their marching columns, were a proud regiment. But none of its soldiers could have been prouder than the small boy who positively worshipped at their parades, became a devout follower of route marches far out into the country and would have given his heart for the privilege of blowing a bugle or beating a drum. Mercifully he had never heard of the words cannon-fodder. All was glamour and glory, from the nodding head of the goat to the silvery jugglings of the magnificent drum major.

To our family fell the duty of billeting a young upper-class lieutenant, a great eighteen stone bag of a man, and his petite, pretty wife. Newly married, they too brought glamour to the house. Wining and dining with fellow officers in the dining-room they produced not only an atmosphere of opulence and aristocracy but also one that until that time had been as foreign to the household as, say, bad language or the smell of opium: the odours of strong drink. It was really a twilight world. While the young lieutenant painfully slogged it out with his men on long route marches, his tender feet unequal to the task of supporting so vast a frame, his attractive little wife sat at home and, after the fashion of the day, painted in water colours. And sometimes, when both were out, I used to creep into their room and lift the lid of the long black tin box and gaze down at the glittering grandeur of an officer's wardrobe, from the finery of mess kit to the flashing gleam of scabbard and sword.

Soon the obese young officer was to be killed in the filth that was Flanders and the babbling Welshmen were to be replaced as cannon-fodder disguised as symbols of glory by men of the Yorkshire and Lancashire Regiment, at whose feet I worshipped with renewed devotion. It was their lot to be massacred in due course in the holocaust of the Dardanelles, far from the pubs and fish-and-chip shops of home. Often I wonder now what the thoughts of the cannon-fodder were, though I knew of no such wondering then. All was still glory:

blow, bugles, blow, swing, rifles, swing. As I listened to the music of marching feet I longed, always, to be a soldier.

Instead of which, in the spring of 1916, as I have already indicated, "the divinity that shapes our ends' rough-hew them how we will", decided to take another and decisive hand in my affairs.

CHAPTER
EIGHT

I was now almost eleven and the time had come for me to take an examination for a scholarship. Not more than half a dozen of us were chosen for the privilege of sitting for this and it is notable that all these came from homes whose heads "were notch above a tapper". The unwashed were also, I fear, the unprivileged. Not that being deprived of the opportunity of sitting for a scholarship was necessarily a deterrent to progress and success. I can recall half a dozen of my 1916 contemporaries who, though leaving school at thirteen, later proceeded to set up successfully in business, often to make sizable fortunes. The mere acquisition of a little learning is not by any means all, dangerous though it may sometimes turn out to be.

Of the written part of the scholarship examination I now recall very little, except that it took place at Wellingborough, to whose celebrated public school I hoped later to go. My recollection of the oral part is much sharper. This took place at Northampton, to where, on a torrid summer day, my father and I went by train. After some delay and difficulty we managed to discover the place of appointment in a back street, by which time, perhaps because of the heat of the day, I felt nervous and flustered. In due course I found myself in an upstairs room, confronted by a bevy of solemn-looking gentlemen who proceeded to ask me a number of questions, all of which with one exception have faded from my mind. This solitary one demanded to know what would happen if a spray of blackberry flowers were covered, throughout the time of flowering, with a muslin bag. I replied that I thought there would be no blackberries because all means of fertilisation, such as bees, would be excluded, but whether this was the correct or expected answer I shall never know.

In due course the list of successful examinees was published and to my utter chagrin and bitter disappointment my name was not among them; I was the only one who had failed. Bang went my dream of going to a public school but far more difficult to bear was the bruising blow to my pride. I had sallied into the lists with a certain degree of confidence, duly supported by my teachers, and I now felt I had received a cruel and startling sock in the eye. My grandfather's old country adage that I had "something in my head besides lice" now echoed about me like a piece of empty boasting. I believe that for many days I was very near to tears.

I had, however, reckoned without "the divinity which shapes our ends". Clearly it was not part of its plan either that I should win a scholarship or go to Wellingborough; another and far more influential pattern had been prepared for me. In due course this was revealed in a letter delivered on an August Sunday morning — even in the darkest hours of the war we still had a Sunday morning post — wherein the County Education

Authorities were pleased to inform me that I had been granted something known as a "Free Place" at the Grammar School at Kettering. "Free" meant free tuition and free railway fares. My pride was restored.

In 1934 Graham Greene got together about twenty celebrated young writers, most of them even more celebrated now, to contribute their impressions and recollections of school-days to an anthology called *The Old School*. The Schools ranged from Eton to a Salford Council School; Harrow to a Lancastrian School in Cork; Wellington to Cheltenham Ladies' College; Berkhamsted, Graham Greene's own school, to Kettering, my own. The writers included Auden, Spender, Harold Nicholson, Elizabeth Bowen, Anthony Powell, William Plomer and others of equal distinction. Looking back over these pieces today I observe that my own is largely a discourse on disillusion, a feeling to which I still subscribe, and that I attribute this largely to the war but equally to the fact that a certain romantic streak in my boyhood temperament had led me mistakenly to suppose that life at a Grammar School would be as different from life at a local elementary school as life in Windsor Castle differs from life in a council house. In other words I had dreams of grandeur which were unfulfilled and it was without doubt this strong and early disillusionment that resulted in my new status being, for a time at any rate, frustrated and unhappy.

There were of course some singular differences between my old school and the new; but in one respect war had affected them equally. The destruction of cannon-fodder now being on the vast charnel-house scale that it was, killing and maiming men by the million, it was a natural consequence that there should be a great shortage of male teachers and a corresponding increase in the number of women occupying the teacher's desk. But whereas this was something that in no sense bothered me at the elementary school I was presently to find it a source of extreme irritation at Kettering. I am now disposed to think that this in all likelihood has something to do with puberty; up to the age of twelve or so it would seem not unlikely that a boy welcomes and indeed relishes a certain maternal touch in the attentions of a schoolmistress. But at fourteen he himself is about to become a man and it is to men that he then begins to look, in my opinion, for greater guidance. At Kettering, until at any rate, we looked in vain.

Again, in these early years, I was not only disillusioned; I was also the victim of extraordinary sensitivity and abysmal shyness. I was so shy that at first I could not face the communal dining-room; my mother packed me midday meals of sandwiches and pasties. Nor, for an agonised period, could I face morning prayers; with trembling and sweat I would hide myself in a class-room until the daily ritual was over. This is not to say that I was in any sense a namby-pamby. I was very fond of, and very good at, football, playing for my 1st XI at the age of fourteen and occasionally for my town XI at eighteen; I loved both cricket and tennis; I became a very fast sprinter, at one time collecting prizes in both the Open and Under-15 100 yards in one afternoon. It was simply that a great sensitivity of temperament was there and as yet there was no adult cloak to protect it. There was, however, an adult hand in readiness to bruise it and bruise it presently, indeed, it did.

The hand was that of Scott, the headmaster. I am fully aware that my comments on Kettering in Greene's anthology *The Old School* aroused consternation, ire and indeed wrath in certain devoted Kettering breasts when the book first appeared. I cannot help this; the experiences of others are not mine; my eyes and mind record for themselves, unaffected by the prejudices of others. (*Apropos* of this, my mentor Edward Garnett used to tell a story of D. H. Lawrence, whose sister came once to see E.G., begging him, "Oh! Mr Garnett, could you *please* make D.H. write like other people?") I am, I am afraid, unable to observe like other people; I am content to observe in my own way. Others among my school-fellows may have been less sensitive, and perhaps for that very reason less observant, than I; they may also have been less prone to be victims of an acute sense of injustice. I do not know. What I do know is that one day when I was in the fourth form I was suddenly summoned to Scott's study, without being told why, there to be immediately and relentlessly whipped, also without being told why. Now I believe that children do not resent punishment, provided they are first told what the punishment is for and secondly that the cause of the punisher is at least reasonably just. Scott, who had neither the wit nor the perspicacity to grasp this elementary truth, accordingly behaved with dismal, orgiastic, lamentable stupidity. I was stunned and lacerated by a monumental sense of injustice; for some hours I actually lost my power of speech. It was only some considerable time later that I discovered that my heinous, hideous, impossible crime had been to allow a dumb, dull class-room neighbour to crib a single sentence from me at a weekly exam. By then, however, it was too late for reparation. The damage was done; the foundations of an implacable hate relationship with Scott had been laid.

Auden, in his piece on Gresham's School, then a very modern one, has something to say about schoolmasters. "I have no wish to belittle a profession to which I have the honour to belong . . . At the same time if one were invited to dine with a company representing all trades and professions, the schoolmaster is the last person one would want to sit next to . . . far, far too many are silted-up old maids, earnest young scout-masters, or just generally dim." Scott, in my view, should never have been a schoolmaster; Scottish himself and therefore prone to call us "byes", he would have made a good civil servant. But the attributes that make good civil servants do not, alas, necesarily make good schoolmasters. Small, bald, fussy, interfering, a tireless busybody, he trotted about the school with what he no doubt hoped was headmasterly dignity, only to achieve precisely the opposite effect.

"If we owe regard to the memory of the dead," said Dr Johnson, "there is yet more respect to be paid to knowledge, to resolve and to truth", and I am aware of course, as I have already said, that Scott served in extremely difficult, not to say distressing, times. He had never more than two or three other male teachers to help him; other possible candidates in that direction were being shot. We were left with what my grandfather, with his usual truthful forthrightness, would have called females; and very female and formidable most of them were. We were either in the charge of tall, gangling, large-breasted women whose thoughts, I fear, were often on subjects far removed from geography; little bouncy ladies of whose virginity there was little question; stern angular mentors, some of them horse-women, of whom it was possible to doubt if they were, in fact, even female. It must be remembered here that men were not only becoming very scarce as schoolteachers; they were becoming very scarce, as one of the lady contributors to *The Old School* points out, for women too. The disturbing day of the low-necked dress had accordingly arrived and one of our female staff would often stand in front of us and, with what object I do not know, idly caress her large breasts backwards and forwards in her silk blouse, perhaps in gentle reference to the peaks of the Himalayas, the importance of whose dizzy heights she was trying to communicate to us from the blackboard. The ascent of high mountain peaks by men, is, as I understand it, of deep sexual significance; and I am not surprised.

One of our male teachers was a certain Mr Gaul. A Yorkshireman, already past sixty, brother of a composer named A. R. Gaul who had written a number of Oratorios, Mr Gaul had come out of retirement to teach us scripture and Latin. A short man, white-bearded, poor-sighted and slightly deaf, he was ripe prey for that particular brand of mischievous persecution that only schoolboys know how to administer. The result was that my Latin was atrocious and my Scripture about as bad. Indeed I have a strong impression that at this time — I am writing now of the last year or so of the war — I was not very good at anything, except perhaps painting and drawing, of which I had always been very fond. Subjects such as trigonometry, mechanics and chemistry were totally beyond my comprehension; I was hopeless at carpentry; I do not recall any particular interest in literature. I was filled in fact with a vast apathy, so much so that I was presently guilty of the unpardonable folly of cutting football, for which I was whipped again and this time justifiably.

How long all this might have gone on and where it might have ended it is impossible to say; but fortunately the hand of "the Divinity which shapes our ends" had not finished with me. Indeed it was almost ready to play not one card in my favour, but two. One such stroke of fate in the year 1919 would have been miraculous; two were to provoke nothing short of a revolution.

But before I divulge these matters it is necessary to go back to my grandfather and his fields, to what was virtually the last golden phase of pure childhood.

CHAPTER
NINE

It was my grandfather's practice to buy up, every summer, a small orchard or two, and occasionally even a solitary tree of plums or pears from some private garden whose owner had neither the time nor inclination to pick the fruit for himself. Of the solitary trees I most vividly remember a tall conical-shaped tree of small honey pears, ripening in August, that grew in an old stone-walled garden side by side with Chichele's charming small grammar school, (see page 35), now used for sacred purposes rather than the secular ones for which it was intended six hundred years ago. The tree not only appeared to me very tall and the pears of a singular juicy sweetness, but the whole garden must have made on my young mind an impression at once permanent and endearing, for it is from this garden and its adjoining stone house that the tragic heroine of *The Sleepless Moon*, a novel of mine written more than forty years later, walks to her wedding in the neighbouring church and subsequently to a marriage unconsummated.

There is little doubt, however, that the sweet honey pears and I were consummated all right. I never knew the name of that pear and I daresay it has long since passed from the lineage of peardom. But its nature in bearing was so prolific that not only did we spend days gathering it for filling skips, baskets, boxes and trays, but it also positively rained in full ripeness from heaven, covering the long uncut grass beneath, the rotting pears themselves being covered in turn by buzzing flotillas of wasps, at which my grandfather swung an infuriated cap in the hot August sun.

Some distance away, across the square, in a short stone side street, we bought from time to time the fruit of other trees, but here in the old back garden of the coach-builder's yard, it is not the trees I remember. No solitary tree of pears, like a honeyed spire, grew there to let imagination feed on its memory until the nettle of tragedy at last grew out of it. It is the coach-builder and his art that I most vividly recall. The essence of it all is as remote from our jet-driven world as the chariot making yards of Rome or Baalbeck, where the underground stables are huge and expansive enough to contain a fleet of a thousand buses.

But here, in this quiet, sycamore-shaded yard and street, there were neither chariots nor buses, but only everyday vehicles of both great beauty and utility, all built lightly but for strength, spokes and shafts and rails all varnished and fined down until they looked not unlike the moulded and twisted sticks of rock — spit-rock, we always called it from the habit of its makers of spitting on their hands as they pulled at the malleable ropes of sugar — we bought at feasts and fairs. Traps, buggies, milk-floats, brakes, butchers' carts, bakers' carts, wagons, wagonettes, landaus, cabs, flies, carriages of ultra elegance: all were there, finished, half-finished, shining with paint and varnish, drying in the sun. No other craft, I suppose, ever contributed so much elegance and colour to the streets of this century as that of the coach-builder. Red, blue, yellow, green, gold, black and even white: the dashing vehicles, still chariot-like, still had the streets as their own. The careering traps, drawn by high-steppers, the comforting beer-barrel buggies drawn by Shetlands, the vast brewers' drays, the double horse delivery trucks, the charging milk-floats glistening with churns of brass and silver finish and those gracious landaus and wagonettes in which, according to class and income, you rode out to relish the summer air.

The first serious accident I ever saw in a street was between one of these vehicles, a two-horsed wholesale fruiterer's truck, and an early motor-car: an event at once shattering and prophetic. The fruiterer and his truck still regarded the streets as the horse's own and unviolated race-track. Like milk-floats, traps and of course fire-engines, they drove everywhere at a pace fearful and swaggering, often in swanky, cocky rivalry. For the fruiterer to meet head-on, at a cross-roads, a totally unexpected horseless carriage stinking of oil and petrol must have been a shock even greater than that of being offered a glass of milk at *The Green Dragon* in place of a pint of porter. But the struggling, bleeding, screaming horses of that Edwardian morning were not merely victims. They were omens; their day of elegance and street chariot-racing, like that of the coach-builder, were about to become part of a vanished world.

The tall conical pear tree, like a sweet shadow of the adjoining church-steeple itself, together with the coach-builder's yard and its gay vehicles and apple trees, were only part, and that an irregular one, of my grandfather's small summer adventures in the world of fruit. Apart from these minor affairs we had a far larger and more permanent piece of business to conduct in that direction. Every summer, I imagine about the first or second week of July, when honeysuckle, hedge roses, meadowsweet and that particular variety of willow-herb known as codlins-and-cream filled every dyke and hedgerow with the full flower-vintage of high summer, we harnessed the horse-and-trap — I had already mastered the business of putting on bridle, collar, belly-band and all the rest — and set off on a journey that for me was like a pilgrimage to Mecca.

If the day were very hot — and in recollection every day was hot — I cut a branch of ash leaves to stick in the horse's bridle in order to keep the flies away. Everywhere fields of wheat, early oats and barley were beginning to show that magical midsummer transformation of colour from pure green and blue green to a vaporous touch of gold. A little late hay would perhaps still lie in the meadows waiting to be carried: the air in consequence full of the scent of it, mixed with the fragrance of honeysuckle and meadowsweet and an occasional pungent pong as the horse broke wind. I must confess that I loved the horse to break wind, especially when trotting. Both high and low notes punctuated one another until, not knowing what was next coming forth in this natural horsy symphony, my grandfather and I rocked about in a state of equally boyish hilarity in the seats behind.

Our destination was the village of Stanwick, the church spire of which was one of the nine we could see from our little farm-holding on a clear bright day. Beside the church the road wound upward on a short hill and then straightened out again. About half a mile along this road stood a four-square house of no particularly great age or architectural style, built of that warmest pleasant limestone that runs diagonally right across England from Wansford (the Wansford-in-England as the legend has it) to the Mendips in the West. The house, its windows often curtained or blinded against the July sun, had an air both unadventurous and respectable. It was a sort of curate's house, in which you could imagine a young, respectable and rather seedy prelate either writing dry, desultory notes for a sermon or making ginger-and-rhubarb jam.

The trap having been brought to a standstill, the horse nodding its crown of ash leaves against the flies, my grandfather would hand me the reins and tell me to hold hard for a jiffy until he went to see if "the old tit" was about.

In the front garden, every bit as respectable as the imaginary curate himself, grew a green-flowered rose. I have never seen a green rose elsewhere and it remains for me, to this day, a kind of hall-mark. It was, it seemed, the only green rose ever raised or grown anywhere and in addition to being a hall-mark it also implanted itself in my mind as something of a miracle. It had, it appeared, been the hybridising crown of the deceased husband of "the old tit", whose presence in the house my grand-father presently came back to announce as confirmed.

We then drove the trap through the front gates, up a short gravel drive and so to the back door of the house. Immediately an astonishing pandemonium broke out. The earth suddenly opened up, like an underground kennel, and let forth a bewildering army of dogs, some small, some large, some puppyish, some almost drunkenly fat-teated, all barking and yapping in what seemed to be quarrelsome savagery at once. The possible effect of all this on the horse being un-predictable — we once had one who would stand vertically on its hind legs, like a fighting stallion out of a picture by Stubbs, at the mere distant sound of the band of the Royal Welch Fusiliers — that my grandfather instantly seized the bridle, leaving me still in the trap, in a state of near paralysis, fear and wonder, not daring to alight in case my legs were chewed to the bone.

"Oh! the dear things won't hurt you. They won't hurt you a bit. They're *pleased* to see you. They're really *ever so* pleased."

With these words, or some others of intentionally equal comfort, "the old tit" doddered forth. Her tiny frame quaked like totter-grass from head to foot. I see her as a kind of brownish, diminutive nun, untouched and unprotected, except for her countless dogs, from the sterner, predatory world outside. Woe indeed, wet or fine, was her recital of lamentation.

Its most consistent text was that of "scrumping". The garden, as I was to discover, was wandering and extensive. Its surrounding stone wall, blessed with fan-trained trees of peaches, plums and even apricots, was not in fact a protection at all but, as walls have so often proved to be in the course of history, a medium of defence merely offering challenge to an invading enemy.

"The boys have been over the wall again, Mr Lucas. There isn't a thing left. Not a cherry nor a gooseberry. I think the currants have all gone too. It's too terrible, Mr Lucas, it's too terrible, Mr Lucas, to think of —"

By now the dogs had quietened. They merely snuffed around the trap wheels. I was able to alight. My grandfather, by nature imperturbable, had little to say by way of comfort and merely puffed at his pipe instead; and since one of his favourite stories was of a day in his extreme youth when he had scrumped a considerable quantity of apples and had hidden them in the furrow of an adjacent ploughed field in the twilight and had then considerable difficulty in finding them next morning, I had every excuse to be quiet too.

The old tit now led us forth, more than ever tottering, to the doomed areas of destruction, the scorched earth left by scrumping boys. The snuffing dogs followed. A path bordered by bush-trained apples and pears, under which grew wild sowings of seeding honesty and golden marigold, together with marrows already as fat as sucking pigs, led away into the distance that seemed to be an even denser forest of plums, apples and pear trees of positive grandeur. The June drop had passed; on all sides the trees were loaded with already fattening fruit. Here and there vast umbrellas of rhubarb leaf, waving beds of asparagus, silvery forests of seakale and mauve lakes of potato-flower proclaimed that the garden was as richly productive at earth level as in the balmy sky above.

We paused, nevertheless, for constant, twittering complaint. What the boys hadn't robbed the birds had. Fat golden and red jewels of ripening gooseberries, scarlet pearls of red currants, positive rosaries of black currants, shining as dark grapes, grew in healthy splendour, the bushes shrouded in old lace curtains, discarded antimacassars and even shreds of female underclothing, everywhere. My mouth watered at the sight of this luscious harvest as frequently as the old tit doddered and twittered in misery. Even today, fifty years later, the squash of a ripe red gooseberry and its seeds against my tongue are enough to recall the contradictory scene of riches and destruction.

Presently and inevitably we were escorted to the front line, the wall, the tragic breach in the defences.

"This is where the boys come over, Mr Lucas. You see where they've broken it down. You can see where they've broken the stones away. Look at the apricots — All broken down —"

My grandfather sucked at his pipe. Like me, he looked in sympathy, but in vain, for a hole in the wall, a displaced stone or two. As for apricots, my young quick eyes could see them hiding, young too as yet, unblemished behind the leaves, snug against the wall.

"It's awful, Mr Lucas. Every year it gets more awful. I'll have to have barbed wire put all along —"

Hereupon my grandfather would shout that all was well. There was nothing to worry about. Boys would be boys.

Deafness not only defeated him. It merely served to heighten the wail of lamentations. The sudden increase

in twittering and tottering always seemed to me that the old tit was about to fall apart.

At some point just beyond this — later in the summer I was forbidden on pain of death ever to go within visual distance of the apricots, the crown jewels of the September scene — the wall took an abrupt turn to the right. The entire garden opened up into a semi-wilderness. The grass was long and unmown, dissected only by a narrow path along which, in single file, the dogs, in pup or not, waddled like an advance party of brown troopers. Abruptly, to the left, there was a sudden drop of twenty or thirty feet into what had once been what my grandfather would have called, and indeed did call "a stun pit". From here, I gathered, had been quarried the stone for both house and garden wall. The calcarcous nature of the remaining soil being admirably suited to the growing of fruit, especially stone-fruit, among which apricots demand certain exceptional conditions, the late husband of the old tit, who I gathered had made a modest fortune from the invention of some patent lamp or other, had everywhere planted fruit with great prodigality.

The result was that the old tit was now the possessor of a positive forest of fruit that she had no idea what to do with. Hence the presence of my grandfather and I to survey and assess the prospect of harvest. The scene was utterly idyllic. Time had covered the lacerated cliffs of stone with grass and thyme and wild rose and elderberry and odd bushes of hawthorn; above it all rose the many fruit trees in their full bearing and prime, in particular pears of many varieties, Blenheim Orange apples,

Worcester Pearmains, Cox's Orange and an apple that my grandfather called "a summerin' apple", on account of its earliness, softness of flesh and inability to keep. This, I fancy, was ready to pick, a pleasant pale yellow in colour, by the end of July, to be followed a little later by that queen of plums I have already mentioned, the squarish apricot-like plum of incomparable flavour always known as the Stanwick Plum (has it died too with the vanished world, I often wonder?) and then in succession the many pears, the russets, the Williams Bon Chrétien, Conference and that great lady, Marie Louise.

But in July the prospect of garnering all these was still well ahead of us. Before that time the boys, naturally, would be over the wall again; blackbirds would have been feasting; the annual invasion of wasps would have begun; summer gales would have ripped off the little remaining fruit; there would be little or nothing left. Nevertheless some assessment of ultimate harvest, pitiful though it might be, had now to be made; a gamble, a bargain, had to be struck.

In uncertain procession, dogs and all, we returned to the house. My impression is that, except when it rained, I remained outside, torn in temptation by ripening gooseberries and currants on the one hand and the cherry trees, of which there were few, on the other. It was only on really wet days that I was invited into the house, my recollection of which does nothing to disprove my impression of the old tit as a brown, diminutive nun. There lingered about the cloistered rooms an air at once ecclesiastical, stuffy, sun-baked and deeply redolent of paraffin. A few cases of stuffed birds, a fox and a stoat

96

or two; whatnots overladen with china; a bewildering variety of chairs, stools, *prie dieux*, sofas and footstools covered either with beads, antimacassars or both, and a great gallery of photographic enlargements of Victorian gentlemen of stern and bewhiskered demean who appeared to be about to preach at me long sermons either on the evils of childish interruption in the world of adults or the rewarding piety of silence: this was the pattern of every room, overlaid even to my childish mind with an air of unhappy solitude.

After what always seemed to me a whole era of pain, the bargain between the old tit and my grandfather was finally struck. I had never the remotest idea of what sums were involved; I only knew, even then, that my grandfather's immense and inborn honesty made him utterly alien to the prospects of sharp practice. It is more than likely that the first bargain was of a preliminary nature, still guided by the prospective disasters of predatory boys, wasps and summer thunderstorms, and that the final one was struck and sealed only when the last Blenheim Orange had been borne home in the September twilight, to be stored on the floor with a thousand others in the little back bedroom where I always slept: a room of which I shall have something of singular interest to say a little further on.

A glass of home-made wine, most probably of elderberry or rhubarb, was the final signal that all talk of importance for the day was over. I always watched it disappear down my grandfather's throat — my impression is one of abstinence on the part of the old tit — with much relief. My own rewards were infinitely less generous.

"Would the little boy like an apple or something?" the old tit always asked and in due course a handful of blackbird-bitten cherries, a pear full of wasp-craters, a bruised and fallen apple or two were, in their seasons, my rewards from the old tit's tottering but affectionate hands. It was indeed good fortune that I had taken the precaution of filling my pockets with choicer, sounder fruit long beforehand. Boys, indeed, will be boys.

In due course, when we returned at some time in early August, it always seemed to me that the depredations of boys, birds and wasps had been of little account. Memory of course tends to count the good, happy years; less often the lean, bad ones. Clearly there must have been summers of disappointment and disaster. One good raging August storm, with clouds sailing in from the West like blue-black tornadoes, would wreck the Blenheim Oranges, the Doyenne du Comice and Cox's Orange, leaving underneath the trees a desolate battlefield of fallen fruit. But time on the whole paints out such dreary landscapes, leaving canvases cleaned and ready for light always brilliant, sun always warm and even torrid and trees always laden with fruit in spite of wasps, as in a promised land.

The great mystery and inquiry in my mind was how we ever managed to find time not only for the garnering of this harvest but for that of wheat and barley too. The journey from home to orchard — there were two choices of road, top-road and bottom-road — alone took an hour, very often more if we chanced on some acquaintance, some road-side stone-breaker, a scytheman at work beyond a hedgerow, a drover wetting a rough whistle on an outdoor settle at a pub. Even in conversations notable for dialogue cryptic, undecorated and dry these exchanges seemed always to go on an unconscionable time.

"Ow bin then?"

"Mid."

"I 'eered talk as she wadn't very grand."

"Bad a-bed and wuss up."

"Old gal come down yit?"

"Fourteen. Last Sunday. Laid on two on 'em though."

"Swine fever over at Long Leys, I 'eered."

"So I 'eered."

"Well, we'd better be gittin' on, else it'll be bull's noon. Giddup there."

"Too right. Be the way, how's Joe?"

"Gone. Took Monday, gone Wednesday."

"Never? If it 'ent one thing it's another."

"Too right. Giddup there."

The entire long day was otherwise ours alone. The only other help on which my grandfather could count, besides Smack, was from that of a rather rapscallion of a character named Sam, the farmer next door to us. Compared with our puny holding his could truly be called a farm: five or six fields, horses, cows, bullock-yards, binders, wagons. Proud as any coachman in livery I used to drive these wagons, full or empty, at harvest-time, handling the big shires as I manfully chewed a straw. This system of neighbourly exchange always worked well at harvest and again at threshing time and even again at ploughing time, when we imported on to that intractable gut-lugging clay of ours two monsters in the shape of great steam engines, one stationed at one headland of a field, one at the other, the plough being drawn back and forth on a long steel coil between. You might as well ask to see a Roman chariot at Ascot or a Christian-eating lion at a base-ball field as ever to see this piece of agricultural antiquity again.

Sam, who had served as a soldier in India and on the North-west frontier, might have come straight out of Kipling. His slightly swaggering, bantering manner, his capacity for beer, his rough warmth, his ability to make every syllable of reminiscence about India and the Army sound like a raging lie made my grandfather's homely innocence seem almost the equal of mine. He and my grandfather always called each other "shop-mate", an echo of the old shoe-making days. When wet weather drove us indoors they sat on sacks of potatoes, bales of straw or even on the chaff-strewn barn-floor and argued of this and that in terms almost revolutionary, blew vile tobacco, released frequent and uninhibited crescendoes of wind and spat, while I, the little pig with big ears sat, looked and listened.

To this scene, inhabited otherwise only by Sam's wife, son and daughter, there came, in I suppose about 1916, a stranger, a figure of touching innocence in the shape of a piece of German cannon-fodder who had mercifully escaped the holocaust of the Western Front (a certain distinguished soldier politician, writing of a mid-war dinner at Brigade H.Q., at which the customary soup, fish, entrée, roast, sweet, cheese, savoury, Moselle, Claret and brandy had been served, subsequently made the comment in his own reminiscences: "Not at all a bad dinner, when you think of it, only twenty-five miles behind the front line," a remark I have always thought must have pleased Siegfried Sassoon and the author of *Good-bye to All that*): a pitifully young German prisoner of war.

Johann had no English. His only means of expression was in the form of a slow, bemused, painfully bewildered smile. Truly Nordic, fair, transparently blue-eyed, gentle, he worked dutifully in a dumb world until gradually, sitting in barns or on wagon-boards, I taught him a few rudimentary words of English. Perhaps it isn't altogether odd that I should remember Johann with such clarity and some affection, since I have over and over again been convinced that this young fair pawn, one of millions moved remorselessly hither and thither in a bloody game of chess, sowed in my mind the first of my doubts on war's futilities. We all grew very fond of Johann and he of us; and later, not long before the carnage of another game of chess was about to be repeated, I painted his portrait in a story, *The Hessian Prisoner*.

It would be late September, sometimes early October, before the last of the apples were gathered in. The leaves of the pear trees were already turning to their rosy-walnut, garnet-golden, vermilion-brown. On some dark-ening evening, with light balloons of mist collapsing everywhere on the wide stretch of river valley, we would drive home with the last truckload of fruit, I as usual blessed with the old tit's parting gift of a few mouldy failings but heavily laden pocket-wise with the choicest prizes I could find. On our way we would pass the big stone water-mill where later on we would bring our wheat for milling, the flour in turn to be baked into "mucky bread". The sound of the mill-race and the grind of truck wheels on the stones of the long hill out of the valley were almost the last sounds (except my grandmother's irate "I'll be burned if you'll sleep in my sheets with that neck. You'll be sowing carrots in it next") before I fell asleep, dog-tired, in the little back bedroom.

All winter that small room smelled of apples, ripe and sweating and laid out on chests-of-drawers, tables and floor for keeping. The only window faced north-westward, over the river valley. On winter nights the great glow of iron-ore furnaces lit up the distant sky with a crimson-golden glow. On the mantelpiece of the fireplace, where no fire was ever lit, a few flower-painted trinkets and Victorian china figures stood with a brass candle-stick. But as if in anticipation of a fire there stood ready in one corner of the room my grandfather's entire gear as a fireman: great brass helmet, boots, axe, belt, rope and uniform. Sometimes, safely alone, I used to try on boots and helmet, only to collapse under the sheer weight and size of them.

One winter night I awoke to the startled impression that the iron-ore furnaces were burning brighter than usual. A few moments later my grandfather rushed into the room, dragged on boots and helmet and uniform, grabbed axe and belt and rope and clattered madly downstairs. After some further minutes someone else, my grandmother or my aunt, came in and took me from my bed. I rather fancy I was five. The curtains having been drawn back, I was held at the window to watch the great fire. Less than half a mile away a boot factory was burning with brilliant ferocity. Pretty soon it was threatening a long low row of stone and thatched cottages. In one of these my grandfather had been born and from that same one, on that winter night, he was bearing away a baby in arms.

The Divinity that shapes our ends appeared in fact to be at work again. The baby was eventually to become my wife.

CHAPTER
TEN

If there is one description that occurs more often in the slow progress of my schooldays towards the end of the war it is the single word "apathy"; Mr Gaul, master of Latin and Scripture, further amplified this to "lethargic". Perhaps I am by nature inclined to be dreamy; perhaps it was the war, with its ever increasing pattern of doom, with the long lists of killed, wounded and missing growing ever longer, the shortage of food, the interminable delays to passenger trains so that the vast ammunition chariots from the industrial Midlands and North often delayed my evening homecoming until after nine o'clock; or it may have been the growing squad of schoolmistresses passing on to us, in their man-starved world, their own lethargies and frustrations.

Of mechanics, mathematics, chemistry and so on I knew, and still know, practically nothing. Others might find the mysteries of changing colours in test tubes a sort of magic; to me it was as remote a mystery as trying to read Sanskrit. The simplest explanation of all, perhaps, is that I was merely abysmally bored. So desperate at one time did I become that I joined a voluntary squad of potato pickers, thus exchanging for a few weeks my class-room for the vast acres of the estate of the Duke of

Buccleuch, of which the memory of the great yellowing avenues of elms on misty oyster-cold autumn mornings remains with me yet, more vivid than any chemical formula or any trigonometrical mumbojumbo.

There may be those who deduce from all this that I was not merely bored, but also rebellious. With this I am inclined to agree. I have a notion that it was a sort of inborn cussedness that for example made me take so little interest in Latin, a fact that I now much regret. I have a natural and insatiable appetite for words, not necessarily those of a nature long and abstruse (I run a mile from intellectual swank words such as "esoteric" and "proliferate", which crawl out of their various holes from time to time) and I like taking them apart, as some people do old clocks, to see what makes them tick. The shaky nature of my foundations in Latin here puts me to much disadvantage and I now often wish that I had attended with greater application to the exploits of Caesar instead of lighting outrageous candles on the back row of the fifth form, thus leading the short-sighted Mr Gaul to the confused impression that the sun had suddenly come out with supernatural brightness.

Rebellious, perhaps; unambitious, certainly. My solitary ambition at this time was to become a painter. My father's ambition for me was, I am quite certain, that I should become either a minister of the church or a musician of sorts. It is, however, a sad thing that whereas our family and indeed my own take the very greatest and most affectionate interest in music none of us have ever yet succeeded in performing on or with any kind of instrument, except my father with his splendid bass voice and my younger son, who briefly mastered the euphonium to a point where he could play *A Farmer's Boy* and *Bless This House* with a competence and fervour that on occasion reduced his mother to tears of adoration at school concerts. Alas, I am sorry to say, I followed the general family pattern; crotchets and quavers and clefs and minims meant even less to me than sines and cosines.

But for art I had a genuine interest and appetite; I looked forward to art class as to no other lesson. We were taught by a Mr Gash. In the late Victorian or early Edwardian era Kettering had produced a painter named Alfred East, later Sir Alfred, a performer of conventional competence who had at one time exhibited at *La Nationale des Beaux Arts* in Paris and whose work, I note, is now returning to some favour, as with other painters of his period and kind. Mr Gash, I fancy, had been a pupil of his. A kindly, simple, local man, he had evidently got it into his head that he ought to talk to grammar school boys in an accent other than his own. Thus misled, he constantly beseeched us to bear in mind such rules as "the heighth of the heye". Others thought this funny; I didn't; and for once I was earnestly sitting at someone's feet, waiting to be taught.

Nothing, in those days, gave parents more pleasure than to be able to demonstrate that their off-spring could either paint pictures or play the piano. "My mother," Henry Moore has said, "had no knowledge of art. Like many parents, she thought that whatever I did was jolly good." So with my painting; as I sketched, painted flowers and copied the various classical prints that hung about the house I found myself much praised, so much so that it was strongly hinted that I ought to take lessons (to this very day I am constantly being urged by my family that I ought to take up painting; in answer to which it is quite useless for me to point out that writing is as much a graphic art as drawing and that words themselves are a form of paint). Time and expense, as well as diffidence, precluded any idea that I should seek tuition under Mr Gash; instead I discovered that the eldest of four sisters living opposite our house gave painting lessons and it was to her eventually that I went, with my new box of oils and brushes, to receive lessons at, I think, the princely sum of a shilling an hour. It may well have been less, since it isn't many months since I was told by a painter of distinction that attendance for instruction at Jacques Emile Blanche's studio in Paris at the end of the last century cost half a franc, plus another half a franc if M. Blanche himself gave you a personal hint or two.

The results of my all too brief lessons in painting were remarkable. They are not to be seen in the Tate, the Prado or the Metropolitan Museum of Art, but in my mother's best front bedroom. They are a most extra-ordinary and inimitable pair of pictures, since they are beyond all doubt the two worst pictures ever painted by man. In strict truth, perhaps, I ought to confess that their horrific badness is exceeded by one other, a landscape. When I last saw this masterpiece it was being used by an aunt of mine in the sitting-room grate as a means of keeping soot from falling down the chimney in summertime. When I asked after its origins she replied with immense pride "It's yours! Don't you remember?" Mercifully time had obliterated everything; my career as a painter was long since dead; my final masterpiece was stopping a hole to keep the soot away.

Here, unless it should be thought that my life has been governed by a sort of celestial traffic warden whose inspired duty it has been to prevent me from taking the wrong turning at street lights or one-way streets, I must apologise for yet again drawing some attention to the movements of the Divinity that shapes our ends.

Hitherto, such movements may have seemed to be of relatively small importance. The next were not. Moreover there were two of them; and they took place together.

The war ended. The grey and dismal morning of the official proclamation was as vivid, for me, though falsely, as the golden days of orchard and harvest-field. The church bells in the ancient and structurally unsafe steeple of the church at Rushden, unpeeled in all probability since the relief of Mafeking, pealed gallantly out again, as if to say "We have won. Ring out wild bells! and damn it all." And damned indeed we were to be.

At school there was little or no evidence of any change for a term or two. Then gradually our erstwhile mistresses began to drift away. (One of them at least was well-sculptured and pretty and there used to be stories of favoured members of the upper sixth being invited to her flat to enjoy the seductive solitude of tea and buttered crumpets; but I was too young for that line of luxury.)

Soon we had a staff seven-eighths of whom were men, most of them soldiers from the wars returning but one of them a Welsh International soccer player of much skill who once helped me put the ball into the opposing net eight times for the First XI, for whom I played when I was fourteen. In *The Old School* I have stated firmly that "I believe I still thought of becoming a professional footballer . . . but I longed most of all to leave the place and never see it again."

Then in the autumn term of 1919 the hand of the Divinity moved again and something of a miracle occurred. Our instructress for English, a gaunt, carroty Scotswoman, under whom I had suffered in steadily mute retrogression of interest in that subject, had left us at the end of the summer term. Anything of even the minutest improvement would have been welcome to us as we re-assembled for that autumn but greatly to our surprise (in my case a stunned surprise) there eventually walked into the class-room a young ex-infantry officer who looked, facially, at any rate, as if he had been mercilessly battered by the shovel of a drunken navvy. He also limped; he also had some difficulty in holding the chalk as he wrote on the black-board, a fact not surprising since he had lost three of his fingers. Nevertheless the painful distortions of the face, already showing signs of healing from a sort of disordered parchment map into something recognisably human again, couldn't conceal that here was a very English face, once good-looking and still alert, kindly and unembittered by all that war had done to it. The injuries to face and hands had been caused by a single German hand grenade and the limp in the legs by the presence of uncountable bits of shrapnel, many of whom continued to roam about the flesh for some years to come, now and then appearing on the surface in order to provide some proof of their existence beside pain.

Edmund Kirby, son of a Northamptonshire farmer, has somewhere described, I believe, the hypnotic presence in the class-room of a pair of vividly blue, enraptured young eyes, ceaselessly watching him as he taught. If his own were thus keenly observant those of the young pupil he was watching, also the possessor of a very English face, can only be likened to the "transmogrifying magnifying glasses" whose use was urged by the elder Weller, in Mr Pickwick's unfortunate court case, on Samivel.

If it is possible to change human vision, or at least to waken it, by the stimulus or even shock of a single experience, then this is a perfect example of it. I do not think I am putting it either too highly or fancifully to say that in that one morning in the autumn of 1919 I not only grew up; I grew up into what I was to be. Fanciful as indeed it may sound, I date my literary career from that moment. "Write me," the young ex-infantry officer said to us, "an essay on Shakespeare. I mean from your own point of view. Don't tell me he was born in Stratford-upon-Avon in 1564. I already know that. Don't tell me either that he wrote *Macbeth* or *The Merchant of Venice*. I already know that too."

In case my already expressed self-criticism as the possessor of a rebellious nature may have been misinterpreted as indicating that I was constantly in a

110

state of war against something (though I don't deny that I often am) I ought perhaps to explain here that by rebelliousness I simply mean being told or ordered to do something by somebody in somebody else's way rather than be left alone to do it in my own. For this reason I have never discussed a word of a poem, play, story or novel with anyone before writing it, a process that D. H. Lawrence called "the give away" and which was once excellently illustrated by Miss Rosamond Lehmann, who confessed that whenever she was asked what her next novel was to be about always replied simply "Two women and a man."

Thus left to my own resources, instead of being chivvied about, I succeeded in writing an essay about Shakespeare without mentioning Shakespeare. Whether this was good or bad I have now no notion of knowing. But one thing is quite certain: it was exactly as if, not having run a race in my life, I had suddenly run a hundred yards in ten seconds dead. I suddenly knew, incontestably, that I was or was going to be, a writer. This empowering fact (it belonged neither to the region of hope nor desire but simply *was*) I confided to no one, first because I had as yet no one in whom to confide, though this omission was shortly to be remedied, but also because the outrageous impossibility of such a fact would have seemed as senseless to others as if I had suddenly revealed that I had stumbled on a process of turning strawberry jam into gold.

Secrecy in ambition is a great fertiliser and in secrecy, for a time at least, my ambition flourished. It now seems to me both interesting and odd that whereas I can remember clearly the various examples of compulsory reading I had endured under the stern gaze of the carroty Scotswoman, among them *A Tale of Two Cities* and a whole year, if you please, on *Kenilworth*, I found myself in some confusion in trying to place exactly the first year's reading under Kirby. I am inclined to think that it consisted in some kind of hyper-sensitive diving into a magical hat: a sweep and a whirl that produced Keats, Shelley, Drayton, (*Fair Stood the Wind For France*), Shirley, Herrick, Lovelace, Milton, Chaucer, Tennyson and so on, a great jewelled jumble coming teeming out of what had been, until then, thin, arid air. Of specific books I recall only one, Milton's "a speech for the liberty of unlicensed printing in the Parliament of England": *Areopagitica*.

That book, short though it is, first brought me face to face with the greatness of the English language, so flexible and capable of constant flowering in comparison with the unflowering, grammar-ridden French or the impossible suety garrulity of German; a neatness so ordered and yet musical, so lucid and yet pictorial. As I read Milton's logical but impassioned plea (and it would do us no harm to remember it from time to time) it is not too much to say that I was not only dazzled as by a great vision but that I realized for the first but by no means the last that prose, in our malleable, delicate, incomparable English, can also be poetry:

"I cannot praise a fugitive and cloistered virtue, unexercised and unbreathed, that never sallies forth and sees her adversary, but slinks out of the race where that immortal garland is to be run for not without dust or

heat. Assuredly we bring not innocence into the world, we bring impurity much rather: that which purifies us is trial, and trial is by what is contrary."

Little though such words and their singing order may mean to most of the present generation of young writers, many of whom appear never to have taken the trouble to learn anything of the use of language and who appear to care for nothing but slinging words haphazard on to the paper, apparently at their happiest when using those formerly mostly favoured by thugs and gutter-snipes, they meant a very great deal to me. I believe there was a time when I could very nearly quote the whole of *Areopagitica* off by heart and I had also reached the point where I was going around with the symphonic nobilities of *The Book of Isaiah* pounding away in my head, a scriptural piece of reformation which much astonished Mr Gaul, who had now confessed that he recognised my talents but deeply deplored the misuse of them. "Ah! Bates, Bates," he would say. "You with your gifts, you with your gifts," and then shake his poor patriarchal head, giving the wayward lamb of my talent up for lost.

It is curious that though I was so carried away on the bright flood-stream of English poetry and the poetic prose of Milton and the Authorised Version I had as yet given no conscious thought to the idea of writing verse myself. I have long supposed that poets write not merely with their own and often secret voice; they need a comparable voice, often secret too, to listen to them. That voice, as far as I was concerned, was still missing. The warm, encouraging voice of a schoolmaster, together with a guiding hand, was admirable but not enough. I needed, without knowing it, another voice, together with another volcanic bang of transformation.

Presently, in the late autumn of 1919, these both arrived: in the shape of a girl.

Before I put down a word about the second of these revolutionary influences I ought to say a little of a third. Somewhere about this time there one day appeared on the morning school-train a complete stranger. For some days we spoke of him merely as "the chap in the green cap". As a gang the dozen or so of us catching the early morning train were inclined to be both clannish and boisterous. We sang popular songs all the way to school, among the ditties being one which Anthony Powell was apparently hearing at the very same time at Eton, namely *K-K-K-Katie, beautiful Katie*, together with that moving tribute to young beauty: *The Tender Blossoms on the tree cannot compare with Mary-Ee*. One of our number was also ingenious and daring, preferring very often to spend the journey swinging from carriage to carriage on the outside of the train, hanging on with his nails at fifty or sixty miles an hour, instead of sitting comfortably inside.

But the boy in the green cap, a couple of years my senior, was neither clannish nor boisterous. He seemed to be coolly exclusive, serious, apart. His pale be-spectacled face gave him the appearance of being swotty. He always carried an armful of books in his hand and was always reading, instead of singing, in the train. Soon he had changed his green school cap for our own and soon he and I were walking part of the way home together.

Henry James Byrom was a Lancastrian who had moved from an older and much more distinguished school than our own in the southern part of the county by reason of the fact that his father had died and he was now living with his mother and uncle, who had come to be headmaster of that very same National School where my father had played his tricks so long before and where in fact my future wife was also to spend her schooldays. One of his ancestors had been John Byrom, composer of that Christmas carol still so often sung, *Christians awake! Salute the Happy Morn.* There seems in fact to have been a strong musical streak in the family and Henry himself was musical too.

The pale face and spectacles did indeed conceal a character that was not merely swotty; it was fantastically brainy too. It was also, as it turned out, warm, witty and affectionate. The brains were of the kind that makes off with high honours in exams as easily as most children lap up ice-cream. This did not prevent him from being, like me, a tolerably good footballer and a great lover of music and the countryside and, unlike me, a good amateur actor. He was the sort of young man who inevitably plays the part of Brutus, Richard II and Macbeth in school plays while the Bates of this world hang about at the back of crowd scenes, growling like unfed dogs and now and then crying out miserably *Hail Caesar!* or something of that sort. His scholastic background was unmistakable. In his uncle's house the regular daily newspaper was *The Times*, which Harry read with the solemnity proper to a London club-man rather than a country school-boy, whereas ours, as befitted a good Nonconformist Liberal family, was *The Daily News*. For the rest of his time at school Harry's scholastic lustre outshone that of all the rest of us, until he finally departed for London University under "Old Gollancz" and subsequently to a mastership at Stephen Spender's old school, U.C.S., where Spender confessed in Graham Greene's anthology that his father allowed him sixpence a week pocket money. I can only say here that Spender was lucky. I am pretty sure I am right in saying that I had fourpence, for which I was expected to clean a few shoes and chop a few sticks in return.

But Harry Byrom was, for me, a most lucky turn-up. He was, at that very moment, the very person I needed. His mind, though brainy, was not sticky. In summer we launched out into long country rambles, revelling in the blossoming of bluebell woods, the coming of hay and harvest, the darling buds of May and the beauty of old churches. In the longest days of summer we were up at six, clad in running shorts, ready for a three mile training session. In winter we sang Handel, Schubert, *There was a Lady Sweet and Kind* and *Riding Down From Bangor* at the piano and gobbled greedily at the only musical fare the town in those days had to offer, a choice finally lying between *Messiah* and Haydn's *Creation* on the one hand and *Patience* and *The Pirates of Penzance* on the other. As is the fashion of growing youth we argued with passion and what we thought was subtlety, thinking ourselves great fellows, and looked down on girls, who in those days mostly wore their hair tied in large funereal black bows at the back, as an unfortunately necessary nuisance to be tolerated distantly. It will perhaps complete the picture of Harry Byrom if I say that he read *Ovid* as other boys read Edgar Wallace and was on occasion prone to quote Latin to the summer skies or, if we found mushrooms of incomparable quality on some dewy September morning, address them with Keats' joyous cry, "*Full of the true, the blushful Hippocrene*"!

If you conclude from all this that "the narrow road to a certain demesne of secluded priggishness" was about to open to me you will conclude correctly. Brains are not all; brains, as a critic has recently pointed out with some wisdom, are not for instance necessary for the writing of novels, whereas imagination is; brains may father *The Theory of Relativity* but not Sam Weller. The world of making fiction, which at the time of which I am writing was only three or four years away from me, is not one of mathematical exactitudes or soluble equations, but one of lying and distortion. Art, as Picasso has rightly remarked, is not truth.

Fortunately I was about to be turned from the narrow path leading "to a certain demesne of secluded priggishness" into one as totally different as it was unexpected; a circumstance brought about by a combination of accident and Shakespeare.

I have never been ardently fond of school plays. The painting of scenery, the ramifications of stage-lighting, the dressing up, the learning of long speeches, the smell of dust and greasepaint have always given me a certain pain. Painful too has always been the presence on the Great Night of fond parents, ready with handkerchiefs to suppress stinging tears if a nervous offspring should fail with "the quality of mercy", and adoring young ladies from neighbouring schools worshipping some new and newly-moustached Mark Antony. My heart still thuds for an extremely small boy given the task of entering the stage from the auditorium at the cue, in *Julius Caesar*, of "Here comes one in haste," only to see him fall, at the critical moment, flat on his wretched face.

Nevertheless school-plays, like church and funerals, have sometimes to be compulsorily attended, at least by pupils. What play we were giving in the autumn of 1919 I have now forgotten, but a certain uneasiness in the memory suggests that it may well have been that messy last infirmity of a noble mind, *The Tempest*. Be this as it may, I went to the Saturday afternoon performance with another friend (Harry Byrom being conspicuously on the stage of course) and much reluctance, no doubt thinking of football.

After a few minutes the play bored me. Certain of my friends tell me that when I am bored either by conversation or persons, two pale blinds slowly come down over my otherwise brilliantly blue eyes, success- fully shutting me away. On this occasion the exact opposite happened. In the semi-darkness of the school-hall I was bored but my eyes were opened. I found them constantly drawn not to the stage and the doings of Ariel, Prospero and Caliban, but to the dark-haired handsome head of a girl sitting in the seat immediately in front of me.

It is not too much to say that I was hypnotised by this head and the smallish, dark-eyed face which now and then turned sideways. In the inevitable agony of such occasions I also found myself tortured between the notion that this sidelong movement of the head was either merely casual or that she was covertly and flirtatiously trying to look at me. By the interval I could stand it no longer; I had to know who she was. "She's my cousin," my friend said and it was like the onset of a new disease.

At the end of the play we were introduced to each other; I was dumb-struck and, wordless, duly departed. All that weekend the liquefaction — I humbly borrow Herrick's perfect word from one of the most perfect of all lyrics — of those dark eyes refused to let me rest. I was, as countless generations of men have been before me, a goner, held in the bonds of calf-love. Though we had hardly met, I found myself already tortured by the repetition of such lines as "parting is such sweet sorrow" and "Farewell, thou art too dear for my possessing". Monday and school seemed a million years away.

When both came I got hold of her name and address and, in trembling and trepidation, wrote to her. To my utterly confounded astonishment there came a reply. It was in an envelope, fashionable in those days, lined with deep, rich purple tissue paper. I was addressed as "my dear". The ecstasy of this piece of intimacy immediately drove me into a distracted secrecy; I could speak to no one; I could hardly join in the singing on the train and there are still times when the repetition of Anthony Powell's ridiculous *K-K-K-Katie, beautiful Katie* haunts me almost as much as Purcell's *When I am Laid in Earth*. Indeed if there had been no reply to my

second letter I believe I would gladly have followed the example of that most melancholy of lines.

But there was a reply; we were to meet. We met, as I remember it, in the First Class waiting-room on Number Three platform at Kettering station. There is no practical reason whatever for there ever being erected a plaque on a house in London saying *H. E. Bates lived here*; but if there were any justice whatever in the history of railways and twentieth century novelists there should be a plaque on the door of the First Class waiting-room on Platform Number Three at Kettering station, saying *H. E. Bates loved here*.

Con appeared to me even more hauntingly beautiful, on that second meeting, than at the first. With her black shining hair, her liquid black-brown eyes and her strong well-developed figure, her gym-slip accentuating the shape of her fine young bust, it seemed that Byron's line *She Walks in Beauty Like the Night* was the one most fitted for her. Confronted with this vision, two years older than myself, I was shy, bumbling, stiff and troubled.

We promptly talked, astonishingly, of literature; she loved, it seemed, poets such as Mrs Hemans but also Shakespeare. Indeed she loved all poetry and had herself actually written some. Had I?

Again if there were any justice in the history of twentieth century literature these two words would go down with the immortality of *Et tu, Brute?* and *Dr Livingstone I Presume?* Had I?

No, I said, I hadn't. I had never even thought of it.

"Why not?"

"Well, I don't know — I don't think I could."

"Of *course* you could."

"What makes you think so?"

"Oh ! I sort of *know* you've got it in you."

"How do you know?"

"Oh! you've *got* to write a poem. You've *got* to write a poem for me. Or else —"

This is not, of course, a truthful transcript of the conversation that took place between us but both the sense and tension of it are all there. I say tension advisedly, for, as I was later to discover, this beautiful young girl was also dominant, insistent and a schemer, passionately set on having her own way. I use the word tension because somewhere in that conversation lay a burning threat that if I didn't write her a poem it was more than possible that she would never see me again. The thought was something I couldn't bear.

It might well have been that, in such circumstances, I should have gone flying for solace and inspiration to the Elizabethans, taking something like Suckling's *Tell me not, sweet, I am unkind* as a model or that stricken piece from an anonymous writer of 1658 which starts:

> "Oh! what a pain is love:
> How shall I bear it?

and ends:

> "I cannot work or sleep
> At all in season:
> Love wounds my heart so deep
> Without all reason."

Instead, I did nothing of the kind. I have already

indicated that the outbreak of war had an effect of saddening gloom on me; its end was even worse. Happily my father had neither sister nor brother, and was himself unfit for service, and my mother only one sister: so that from the point of view of wounding or bereaving us we had been spared the more grievous of war's trials. But the effect of those long, black, mortifying lists of killed, wounded and missing that filled column after column of every morning newspaper had made a searing impression on me that has never left me; nor can I ever forget the little improvised street shrines decorated, as one still often sees in little Italian cemeteries, with faded photographs of the dead and a few jam-jars of fading flowers.

Thus affected, I wrote a poem on *The Tomb of the Unknown Warrior*. I suppose it had the piety of extreme innocence about it, but in its way it was not only the first thing I had expressed in verse but probably the most serious I ever was to express in that medium. Shown not only to Con but to Edmund Kirby, it suddenly brought me much adulation.

"*There* — I told you you could do it. I *knew* you could. They're going to print it in the school magazine, aren't they?"

Yes: they were going to print it in the school magazine, that universal graveyard of so many budding poets, and they duly did. For myself it was the first of a host of embarrassments of seeing myself in print; for Con it was a moment of triumph. She basked in reflected glory; I was her discovery.

"You see, I *told* you you could. You've got it *in* you.

Now you've got to write *more* poems. Lots and lots. Promise me. Lots and lots and lots and lots."

It was all rather like being pushed into playing in a football match without knowing anything about the game and then doing a hat trick. Suddenly, ridiculous as it may now seem, I felt myself propelled along by bounding waves of inspiration. Most of this was instigated by Con and *the love that wounds my heart so deep without all reason*, and the rest by the more reasoned sobriety of Edmund Kirby's praise. A man of few words, even to the point of being phlegmatic, sometimes even sardonic, Kirby was by no means an easy mentor to please.

For the next several months I not only wrote poems. Con and I entered into a long and passionate correspondence. Sometimes our letters went by post, at others by less orthodox means. I should explain here that the Grammar School and High School at Kettering in those days were contained in one building, boys in one half, girls in the other. Though this did not mean that we were in any sense a co-educational establishment it did mean that girls and boys perforce shared certain class-rooms though at different times, notably the chemistry labs., the library and the art room, so that it was by no means uncommon for the progress of the boys' upper fifth towards the chemistry lab., on the second floor, to find itself barred on the stairs by the jostling descent of the girls' lower sixth on its way to a lecture on Wordsworth in the library. As a result there was inevitably much confusion, dropping of rulers and notebooks, giggling and a great rustling of paper.

As an echo of all this I recently had a letter from a lady, now in her sixties, who wrote: "I am married to Dickie X., who was one of your class-mates. I wonder if you remember me? I used to carry Con's love-letters to you up the leg of my knickers." So does the romanticism of first love sometimes survive, with at least some little part of it undiminished over half a century.

But it wasn't until the following spring that there occurred the first real moment of conflagration in first love. Con, as I have said, was a schemer, a feminine characteristic not unknown even in school-girls ("Their need is great," I once heard a girls' headmistress say and the words still seem to me to have in them a truth bordering on poignancy) and one of the first of her schemes was to arrange for me to spend week-ends at the house of my friend her first cousin, who lived in the same town a couple of streets away. At first the cousin and his sister, a pretty girl dying of consumption without fully knowing it at that time, used to make a wandering foursome with us to explore the surrounding fields and woods, where wild purple rhododendrons and primroses grew in great profusion. But soon the cousin and his sister were learning to exercise an anti-gooseberry diplomacy, so that Con and I were left more and more to ourselves. This seemed to me marvellous; I grasped at every opportunity of being alone with her, simply to talk of literature, flowers and my new poetry. It was all I needed; I never even remotely imagined that there could be anything more.

One warm fine spring evening we wandered along the wooded banks of a brook, probably a small tributary of the River Welland. Primroses, kingcups, white and purple violets and Shakespeare's Lady-smocks bloomed everywhere about the marshy earth. After some time I stopped to climb a stile and then, suddenly turning my head to look for Con, found myself caught up in an unexpected, swift and passionate embrace, and then kissed long, fully and ardently on the lips.

How I recovered from this totally unexpected but delicious ravaging of my boyhood innocence I find it hard to say; it sometimes seems to me not at all impossible that I might have been left speechless for the rest of my life. There was certainly, at that ecstatic moment, nothing to say; nor could I have said it if I had wanted to; instead I could only offer my lips in further sacrifice, surrendering to an ardour returned by lips ecstatic, compulsive and not wholly inexperienced. It was no longer a question of sweet, devoted friendship; the moment was more like the fusion of two white-hot wires. I was more than slightly shocked and intoxicated in consequence; it was now a case, in Herrick's words again, of:

> "Thou Art my Life, my Love, my Heart,
> The Very Eyes of me;
> And hast command of every part,
> To live and die for thee."

The over-sensitive intimacies of first love demand, as I have already indicated of poetry, a particular kind of secrecy. Any other mundane, time-table ridden, meal-ridden, family-ridden world must be shut out. First love develops in its own sacred, suspended, breathless, often wordless vacuum. It generates, and revels in, its own pain. It has no language of any known syntax or co-herence that can express to others outside the vacuum what ecstasy it feels, always believing that others have either not felt it or not in the same way, never pausing to enquire after the fact, as old and inevitable as dawn, that a million million others have.

So we began to meet in secret, or what we thought was secret: under dark railway arches, in remote woods, in hayfields, under wet oak trees dripping with rain, in railway carriages and inevitably, when all else failed, in the First Class waiting-room on Platform Number Three. (We chose the First Class waiting room because there were never any First Class passengers.) We deluded ourselves that only the most intimate of friends and confidants knew of these things; of course everybody knew. Even the porters at the station knew and occasion-ally came to spy gleefully on us as we were locked in blind embrace in the First Class waiting-room. The masters at school knew. Now, however, I was no longer bombarded in class with sallies of crushing reprimand such as "I see our friend Bates is dreaming again". The approach was more subtle, the sarcasm infinitely heavier. "I see that our friend Bates has his head in the clouds again. No doubt with eyes on something of more pressing importance than the Treaty of Paris." The word "pressing", of course would draw much laughter.

I did not care if Scott knew; but I think Con was perpetually alarmed at the prospect of discovery by her Headmistress, a certain Miss White, of secret meetings in corridors and the passage of *billets doux*: hence the constant need for the clandestine up-the-knickers postal system. On my fourpence a week I couldn't afford many stamps, though Con, who already earned money as a pupil-teacher, my entry into which realm of education would have given Scott so much pleasure, could afford both elegant notepaper and gifts to me of the works of Shelley and Keats richly bound in purple or olive suede at Christmas or on my birthday. In return I once presented her with a sixpenny bar of Cadbury's Milk Chocolate for which I had saved up for three weeks, only to have it rejected on the grounds that I ought not to waste my money. My remorse at such intolerable spurning of my gift was so great that my entire soul was lacerated, a tragedy that didn't prevent my eating the whole chocolate bar myself on my lonely way home in the train.

All this time, egged on by Con and almost silently encouraged by Kirby, who in his wisdom would rather say nothing at all than outrightly condemn or praise, I was writing poetry. That this poetry was infinitely and execrably bad I have now no doubt; mercifully all of it is now lost. A few years later when Edward Garnett had read and approved my first novel, *The Two Sisters*, which I am happy to say is still in print after more than forty years, he asked if I had written much poetry and if so would I send him some. Eagerly I replied that I had indeed and sent off a great batch of adolescent MSS for him to read. Though he had praise for one or two pieces it was not of an exuberant kind. Garnett was rarely wrong in his judgements and I scarcely wrote another couple of dozen stanzas in my life.

128

All this time too my appetite for literature was well served. Not only had I access to the Carnegie Library at Rushden but also to the far larger, far better Carnegie Library at Kettering; I still had my father's books and the contents, modest though they were, of the school library. Somewhere about this time my father had suddenly persuaded himself of the virtues of bribery in relation to my scholastic progress and had instituted a bonus scheme whereby I got £1 for a first place and half that sum for a second place in any subject at the end of term. As I was almost invariably certain of firsts in anything connected with literature or art I sometimes found myself three or four pounds richer when school reports arrived, and with this money I sometimes bought books.

Among them, as I remember it, were *A Shropshire Lad* and Hardy's *Satires of Circumstance* but in case these should seem a rather superior taste for a boy of fifteen I should here add that I still loved the secret readings of *Chips* and *Comic Cuts* which my grandfather and I held as often as possible under hay-stacks or in the tool-shed on wet afternoons, I sitting on the bran barrel as I read out to him the exploits of Weary Willie and Tired Tim and the inhabitants of Casey's Court, he half asleep on a sack of chaff while westerly rain lashed at the cobwebbed windows and the blue tea can hotted up on the paraffin stove. My love of the two comic papers was all the greater because my father, in yet another example of his stringent Methodist rules, had always conceived them to be a source of mischief, if not indeed of downright evil and corruption, and had long forbidden their entry into the house. By contrast my grand-father adored them, reserving for Little Willie and Tired Tim all the adulation he had once given to Little Tich, for whom he had made the renowned long boots, and such Victorian stars of the music-hall as Dan Leno and Marie Lloyd. Pressed by me he would sometimes also sing songs:

> Rollin' round the town,
> Knockin' people down,
> 'Avin' a rare old booze I bet,
> Tastin' every kind o' wet,
> Rollin' round the town —

and sometimes a song of the Irish, *On the Boat that First Took me Over*, some lines of which went:

> They brought me fat pork
> On the end of a fork,
> And said "Paddy, ate that."
> I said "I can't, it's too fat,"
> On the boat that first took me over.

Thus for all my progress towards the first standards of some sort of sophistication I still never lost track with the land, the characters on it and the ripe, rough Midland vernacular. A drover staggering home from market, with burning eyes, three parts drunk, would still stop off at the little farm to tell us a rambling tale or two; we still laid nightly snares for hares in the hedgerows; a convoy of gypsy caravans coming up bright coloured against the skyline would sometimes stop and pass the time of day; my grandfather had nothing but friendliness for gypsies and sometimes one of them, a blind man, would alight and come to greet him.

This meeting always had in it for me a great moment of wonder. One of the more remarkable physical characteristics of my grandfather was that he had a double thumb. This thumb, though congenital, looked as if it had been roughly crushed into twice its normal shape by a heavy press. I used, as a child, to fondle its rough spoon shape with an amazed disbelief. In silence the blind gypsy from the caravan would handle it too. It was a certain sign of recognition between two old friends who hadn't, perhaps, met each other for a year.

"It's George," the gypsy would say. "Old George."

Hereabouts, no doubt stimulated by the slightly older company of Harry Byrom and Con and the encouragements of Kirby, to say nothing of my father's bonus scheme, I began to work harder and with more conscious direction. "I am become a man and put away childish things", is perhaps all too pale and tame a description of the fantastic stimulus of the injection given by puberty somewhere between the ages of twelve and fourteen, possibly the greatest single miracle wrought in man. Growing up, growing pains: these too are descriptions too pale for the sudden upsurgent skylight into adolescence.

But now, also, I had a more practical reason for work. There loomed ahead of me, some time after my sixteenth birthday, the forbidding challenge of what was then known as *The Joint Oxford and Cambridge University Certificate*. It was the sort of thing that Harry Byrom could, and indeed did, dispose of with less trouble than eating toast and marmalade at breakfast. Not so I; many of the defections in my earlier scholastic progress were like old sores — nothing, it seemed, would heal them now. Nor was there any kind of precedence for supposing that love, sweet though it was, would perform some alchemic miracle in the exam. room. I do not waver, and have never wavered, in my belief that love is of far greater and more rewarding importance than trigonometry or calculus, but my position for proving this proposition to either my tutors or the examining magistrates at Oxford and Cambridge was not exactly a tenable one. A pass of some degree of excellence in the Certificate might well mean a passage to University. I had not, at that time, thought about University. As at a meal, I had merely concentrated on getting through the bread-and-butter; the cake might come afterwards.

The summer of 1921 was incredibly long and hot. No rain fell for several months. A summer virtually beginning in February lasted on until November. Great cracks, almost chasms, broke up the clay of harvest-fields. Beans shot from their grilled black stalks like bullets. There were many fires. My grandfather and his fellow firemen, already considerably frustrated by a pair of greys who, somehow sensing fire, always either reared up on their hind-legs or reverted to the disposition of donkeys at the mere sound of the alarm, were further hampered by the fact that the greys sometimes also lay down and then took a good half hour to harness, so that

132

very often the fire was out before the scorching chariot arrived. More often than usual that summer we heard the fire-bell clanking up the road. Instantly scythe and rake and pitch-fork would be dropped as we rushed to harness the horse, just in time to follow the chariot and its fuming greys, now at full pelt, as they passed the farm-gate, the firemen hanging on to the engine and shouting with the enthusiasm of small boys going to a bun fight. Somehow I was always just in time to hang on to the backboard of the truck, eventually to arrive on a scene where the only source of water, a brook, had long since dried up in the drought, and a row of thatched cottages or a couple of haystacks smouldered like black funeral pyres in the intense heat of afternoon.

By July, the time of the exam., the heat was intolerable. Already I had got into the habit of getting up at half-past five or six, both for the purpose of working on old exam. papers in the cool of the morning, and of catching an earlier train in order to snatch a few precious moments with Con. There has always been in my character this strong pull of conscience on one side and a disposition to flout authority and rule on the other. The results of this, call it antagonism or cussedness or what you will, have sometimes been bad; sometimes, on the other hand, good. I think they were good when I was able to enjoy a blessed and secret hour or two with a passionate girl of nearly eighteen in a July meadow, in the shade of a sycamore tree, before the blistering heat of the day began. It helped to take my mind off the exam., and also to soften some of the tensions for an ordeal the outcome of which gave me little hope and even less, I fear, to my mentors.

I was also relieved on the first of those torrid mornings — we were actually allowed to sit in our shirtsleeves, normally an unheard-of thing in those days — to observe that one of Con's sisters, Dora, a pretty girl and already a fully-fledged schoolmistress, was the exam. overseer for the day. She gave me the sweetest of smiles as the exam. papers were given out and I suddenly felt confident and at home. Con was one of a large family of brothers and sisters, mostly older than herself, and one of her brothers had that not uncommon knack of improvising on the piano, which provided him with an evening job in the local flea-pit, pitching in at the right moments with yearning music for love-scenes, desolations in a minor key for the dying and the *Overture to William Tell* for every runaway stage coach and every pursuing cowboy. Whenever we watched the stirring doings of Pearl White, the mad pursuits of the Keystone Cops or the genius of Chaplin and perhaps the even greater talents of Buster Keaton, Con and I sat on the far back seats, pressed in long embrace in the darkness, hushed as always in deep secrecy, she fondly believing that her brother on the piano was a great a genius, though unsung and undiscovered, as Keaton and Chaplin, so that I almost wished, then, that I had learned the piano.

As for the exam., it seemed to me that I did well with all that was connected with Literature; tolerably well with History, Geography and even Mathematics; appallingly with Latin and so blankly and with such negation with mechanics and the sciences that I actually walked out of the exam. room after the shortest permitted span of endurance, on each occasion bumping straight into Scott outside the door, each of us giving the other a glare cold enough to have frozen a polar bear. It seems to me that Scott's pervading fault was contained in a stern Scots inelasticity which, poor man, he couldn't help. I am assured that in the Scottish household of today the man is still undisputed master of it; all others must obey; if the "meister" feels the need of a tonic in the middle of the night and orders "Wumman, get me a wee dram, I dinna feel so good", then the wife too must obey. So with Scott; he seemed to see himself as an instrument whose sole purpose was the creation of an endless line of other school teachers, bank clerks and chartered accountants. These were the ultimate ideals in life and those who obeyed the rules to achieve them were sure of his blessings, dour though it might be. But Scott in his entire career had never come across a pupil who instead wanted to be a writer and he had neither the perspicacity nor imagination to do a sensible thing about it. It was rather like running a school for computer-training, only to find that the sole object of one pupil is to write a *Sonata for Clarinet and Grasshoppers*.

Happily, as the exam. ended, so did term; the hot, blistering summer, however, went on; and soon I was back on baked, cracked stubbles, the great dry beards on the wheat-sheaves rustling like the flare of a suddenly started fire itself, the thistles withered to wands of needles and white down long before the scythe ever touched them. Brooks, ponds and dykes were now all dry; when we went to collect water from the brook we might as well have taken a spoon to collect it in. In the orchard of the old tit there was a mighty murmurous congregation of wasps, so that it was almost impossible to pick a plum without being stung. The garden was parched and flowerless, wholly undecorated except for the ghostly silver pennies of honesty seed, ready to join the floating flotillas of thistledown. But for me, at any rate, it was again all pure joy; blessed by massive suns, the apples, plums and pears tasted more sweetly than ever, and in the heart of such an idyll I quickly forgot school, exams., and the results of exams.

I was therefore stupendously shocked one morning to see Harry Byrom rushing up the garden path to our house, waving *The Times* and crying "Third, old fellow, third, third!" Mystified as well as astonished, I asked what third?

"Honours," he gasped. "Honours. You. Look, it's here in the first column."

Seeing my name in *The Times*, I suddenly felt as if I had been elected Member of Parliament or something.

"No exemption for metric., or anything like that I'm afraid," he said. "Still, you can do metric standing on your head now."

Honours, honours, I kept saying to myself and felt like a strutting but unbelieving peacock.

It is my impression that in those days metric., or exemption from it formed the first necessary passport to university. I was therefore much surprised when, soon after the beginning of the autumn term, my father one day called me aside and said:

"They think you ought to go to Cambridge."

Whether he meant soon or later I was too flabbergasted to ask.

"I've thought a lot about it," he said. "It'll take a lot of money."

How much? I wanted to know.

"Every penny I've got," he said. "Every penny."

Then, I informed him simply and with no hesitation, I wouldn't go.

I have never been sorry about that decision. I have never regretted University. My two sons, offered precisely the same terms, though without the financial stringency attached, in due course made precisely the same decision. Perhaps we are not a university-minded family; perhaps they also incline to the view that scholastic degrees, letters after one's name, the acquisition of much knowledge and a certain social cachet do not necessarily constitute education. I like to think that Renoir, Sisley, Cezanne and Toulouse-Lautrec went to neither Oxford nor Cambridge, Winchester nor Eton. I was far from embittered by the prospect of Cambridge being snatched away from me; I rather welcomed it as a relief from any further exercise in scholastic regimentation and later, not very long later either, was actually glad of it as having been an escape; for by the time I was twenty my first novel was published and only a few years later I had added two or three more books to my name and had begun to establish for myself a certain reputation. My two sons happily followed the same pattern of success; they were sensible enough to recognise that life needs a great many things that a university curriculum cannot teach: which, in the present state of much university unrest and disruption, is perhaps just as well.

But what did embitter me was to be told by my father that since I didn't wish to go to Cambridge I must therefore leave school at the end of term. That was truly the unkindest cut. I was too saddened at the time to reason that since I was still only sixteen I therefore needed at least another two years at school before entrance to Cambridge could be hoped for: all a further drain on my father's pocket, since he had my sister and brother to educate too. One of the troubles with my father was that he had no business brain; he was a pillar of unimpeachable, almost naïve honesty. During the First World War he had seen mushroom fortunes made by boot manufacturers who had no scruples whatever about taking advantage of mistakes by ill-informed government departments or by a sly wriggle or two in the tax net. His strict Methodist conscience would have no part of these things. Yet at the same time, and just as naively, he would weekly enter competition after competition mainly in the new Harmsworth publications, solving ingenious problems, composing ingenious ditties and so on, in the passionate hope that he would one day win £20,000 for himself. I think the most he ever won was a fountain pen. Similarly deluded by some bucket-shop literature about a great new venture in rayon that would make him a certain fortune overnight he had, about the time of the Cambridge project, lost all his spare capital and thereafter, for the rest of his life, kept the worthless share certificates locked in his bureau, for ever hoping that the God whose praises he sang so fervently every Sunday would take a Divine hand in the much needed restoration of their value.

So, having accomplished a success I had never dared hope for, I left school at the age of sixteen and a half. Not only was I young; I was also extremely naïve, extremely gauche, extremely sensitive and still locked in the twin secret bonds of first-love and poetry.

What was I to do? Which way to turn? I hadn't the remotest, vaguest idea.

For several weeks in the New Year I mooched about: waiting, like Mr Micawber, for something to turn up. Even the mere promises of opportunity in a town governed by one staple industry are thin, however, and for some time nothing did turn up. There did come a suggestion that I should apply for a post in the foreign department of a London bank but my father wisely reminded me that such a path could only mean my spending the rest of my life with figures; and I often thanked him for that. As for the staple industry of the town he was still adamant on that score and therefore that path too was closed.

It must have been nearly March before something else turned up and this time it seemed too good to be true. It appeared that a local newspaper, and also a very old one, *The Northampton Chronicle*, was looking for a junior (very junior) assistant reporter for its newly-opened Wellingborough office. Accordingly I was requested to go for an interview one afternoon with a certain Mr Bretherton who could tell me all about it and assess my potentialities. Filled with a glowing belief that a job on a newspaper was surely the way to learn how to write, I duly went along and found myself in the presence of a smallish, fattish man of untidy appearance and slightly alcoholic air. Mr Bretherton was also effusive. He proceeded to instruct me in the wonders of the journalistic world and how greatly they would profit me. I was of course most fortunate, he kept telling me, that this was the spring of the year. The best time was coming. In Mr Bretherton's view nothing could equal the joys to be obtained on the provincial journalistic roundabout, especially in summertime; undoubtedly I should have the time of my life. Fêtes, garden parties, flower shows, tennis tournaments, regattas, Sunday school treats, cricket matches, bun-fights of all kinds: the picture was idyllic. Did I like the thought of it ? If so the job was mine: at ten shillings a week.

I accepted. When earlier I recorded that in the eighties of the nineteenth century my mother worked for two shillings a week it did not at first occur to me that an increase of five times that amount in forty years could hardly be called either progress or munificent. At that time I was far from caring; ten shillings or no ten shillings, I was to be a writer by profession. It was great. It might even be, wonder of wonders, that my work would appear in newspapers. They might even print my poems.

I duly went off to the Wellingborough office, which was just off the old market place, in sight of the ancient Hind Hotel, every morning by train.

Outside the station at Wellingborough there always stood an old green horse bus, in charge of and driven by a rather unkempt, long-coated gentleman who looked for all the world like a seedy descendant of the father of Sam Weller. "Straight up to the town! No waiting!" Passengers, if in ones or twos, might on the contrary wait twenty minutes, or even more, before the driver decided he had passengers enough to make the long uphill trip to the Market place worth while. What his charge was for both journey and waiting time I never gathered; such luxuries were not for me.

Out of my ten shillings I had of course to pay train fares and this left nothing for lunches or even a cup of tea. As a result I had to evolve a special method for actual survival. This meant leaving the newspaper office at 12 o'clock midday, running all the way to the Midland Station at Wellingborough, about a mile out of town, and catching the 12.25 to Rushden. This journey, if the fireman didn't misfire with the transfer key to the branch line at the signal box, took seven minutes. Since the return train left at 1.19 this meant that I had to run every inch of the way home, again nearly a mile, gollop the lunch my mother had waiting for me and then run all the way back to the station again, with about a minute to spare. Small wonder that I was thin as a rake and developed no little prowess as a runner.

The early morning train got me into the office about nine o'clock. An inevitable smoky air of grey dreariness hung over everything. Some of my erstwhile school-fellows, now bank clerks, suitably dressed in bowler hats, pin stripes or smart Lovat checks, had warm and comfortable banks to which to retire for the morning's work. I had a dingy upstairs room with bare floor boards, a table, two chairs and the black basket sort of fireplace you see in Cruikshank's illustrations for Dickens. My first job of the day was to rake out the ashes, go to the cellar for coal and a few broken pieces of old boxes and get a fire on the go. It never seemed to be anything but perishingly cold in that office. While the fire slowly drew up I did my best to keep warm by sweeping the floor, tidying Bretherton's desk and actually doing the sort of exercises, flapping my arms back and forth across my chest, that you still see outdoor workers doing in the dead of winter.

By about ten o'clock it was time to make the first two calls of the day: one to the Coroner's office, the other to the police station. As the Coroner's office was only just round the corner, in the shadow of the church, in a narrow street of black brass-knockered doors that itself looked Dickensian, I almost always went there first. In the hush that pervaded the inside office you could almost hear the scratch of quill pens, again straight out of Dickens. My purpose in going there was to discover if anyone had been murdered, committed suicide or had surrendered life in any other way that called for an inquest. It was very rare that anybody had. Sometimes a man had fallen dead of heart failure in the street but mostly my answer was "Nothing this morning," as if I were the baker, the milkman or the butcher.

I then went to the police station. Not that it matters a great deal now, but I feel bound to record that on the whole the police of Wellingborough at that time, on duty or off-duty, were the most uncouth, most bog-headed, most foul-mouthed collection of humans I had ever met. Later I played several games of football against them.

The air of the dressing-room was a cess-pool of filth calculated to make the language of Newgate gaol seem like the whisperings of a convocation of Sunday-school-teachers. I disliked them for other reasons. One practical joke on a new, young green cub reporter is to be expected; two or three can be laughed off; after that it isn't very funny. One day, inquiring whether an unsuccessful suicide would be charged or not, I was solemnly informed by no less a person than the station sergeant "No. They give them a second chance these days." Another day I was sent traipsing a couple of miles to investigate a fire that never was. Two days later, once bitten, twice shy, I failed to heed the news that a big factory had been burned out the previous night. Naturally it had.

On Thursdays I collected the charge sheet drawn up for Friday's proceedings at the weekly petty sessions. Petty is here the *mot juste*. A drunk or two, a labouring man knocking his old woman about, the theft of a skin of leather from a factory, two schoolboys breaking windows, a case of assault, another of breaking and entering: the petty pattern was invariably the same. Nevertheless I always enjoyed the courts; it was always hard to say whether or not the magistrates were odder than the defendants and I daresay many of them were, in some way or other, just as guilty. It didn't take me long either to detect that the Clerk of the Court had seen to it that most things were carefully cut-and-dried before the court began and had already made up his mind, in spite of much pleading by learned gentlemen for one side or the other, what the result of each case should be. The

144

taste left was unsavoury but in spite of it I scribbled madly away in the reporters' box, my little pigs' ears as sharply open as ever they had been under the wheat stooks in my grandfather's harvest-field.

Another piece of Dickensian survival that I attended was *The Board of Guardians*. This, if memory serves me correctly, met at the local workhouse. If it wasn't quite like *Oliver Twist* it still had about it the old grim air of Victorian charity. A wholly estimable number of middle-class ladies and gentlemen sat about a long mahogany table, armed with writing paper and notes, and discussed for entire wearisome afternoons cases of need and hardship or abuse of both, while I made desultory notes and stared out of the window, imprisoned again, looking for the sun.

Presently it turned out that Bretherton the giver of all good gifts, the barker selling the joys of the summer journalistic vaudeville and roundabouts, was a very different person from the journalist actually at work or under pretence of work at the office. Bretherton, I soon discovered, rarely turned up at the office. When he eventually did so it was in a state of alcoholic stupor bordering on rage or sheer sleepiness. The former usually spent itself on a spluttering lecture to me and my woeful deficiencies ("No bloody good sitting here all day. Got to get out. Got to meet people. Got to *ferret*, see, my boy, got to ferret. The rabbits are out there, boy — got to ferret 'em out, got to ferret 'em out") and the latter in a long deep sleep in front of the fire or with head sunken across his desk. Sometimes too came Bretherton's buddy, his father-in-law, alcoholically embalmed too, so that presently the pair of them were asleep, lost in a happy afternoon duet of snoring so that I, since we had only two office chairs, was perforce pitched into the street.

That I was a very bad reporter was indisputable; I will not even start the pretence that I did my best. I had no best to do. I was revolted by Bretherton and the office; I was bored by visits to confectioners to discover what size a wedding cake had been, how many guests had attended the wedding and what they ate. I was equally bored by brides' mothers, from whom it was my duty to extract lists of presents. This boredom was now and then alleviated by my attendances at the monthly meeting of the County Football Association, at which the chairman wore a strange Churchillian bowler hat which he never took off, and when I was sometimes invited to pick out of another hat the teams competing in the next County Cup draw. These committees were composed of jolly, homely characters, often considerate enough to close their meetings early, so that I should not miss the last train home.

Not only, however, was I bored; I was very lonely. Indeed it would be fair to say that I have never been so lonely before or since that short spell of drab, journalistic penury. I hadn't seen Con for many months and for a good reason. All that time she had been in hospital. Flying along a school corridor at full pelt one day — she was something of a tom-boy — she had put out her hand to hold back a swinging glass door and had slit her arm, and with it an artery, almost from wrist to shoulder. This accident had removed her as completely

146

from my life as if she were dead. I didn't even know the name of the hospital.

Soon April came and with it a new daily nightmare. Early every spring there spreads through the British Isles a disease, a rampant epidemic, known as the flat-racing season. Newspapers are suddenly read as if only horses and their jockeys occupied the universe. Form, tips, runners, prices: millions think of nothing but horseflesh and all that appertains to it. It is a world in which I have not, and have never had, the remotest interest; but suddenly I found myself remorselessly caught up in it. Until that time the afternoon edition of the paper had suddenly turned up from head office by bus, in bundles, like so much waste paper. Now there began to arrive special racing editions, similarly issued by our rivals next door, *The Northampton Echo*, who had what seemed to me an army of swift footed newsboys rushing about the streets yelling what I at first thought was *Sporting Tissue in 'is shirt!* It took my bewildered and innocent brain some time to work out that this meant *Sporting Tissue Edition*. It was my duty somehow to combat this onslaught on the waiting layabouts, dead-beats and out-of-works who mooched and lounged about outside the office as if awaiting news of a dying monarch. All afternoon the telephone rang incessantly. All afternoon I scribbled down the names of winners, runners up, starting prices. Frantically I set them up in type in one of those rubber stamp printing outfits that boys still delight to be given at Christmas-time, banged the resulting lettering (which I only *hoped* was correct) on a purple ink-pad and so to the stop-press columns of

147

mountains of afternoon extras, which in turn were grabbed up by impatient newsboys waiting to join *Sporting Tissue in 'is Shirt* on the streets outside.

If anything was guaranteed to pole-axe my fond notion that working on a newspaper would be a sure way of teaching me to write this was it. Rapidly, for some time, I had been working up a hatred of the dingy office, the weddings, the political meetings, the Coroner's office, the police station, the daily sprint home for dinner, the alcoholic snoring Bretherton and his father-in-law. It now suddenly occurs to me that I have neglected to mention a charming habit of Bretherton's: namely that of spitting into the office fire. In periods of sobriety his aim was occasionally near accurate, sometimes actually accurate. A brief sizzle on the hot coals indicated a bull's eye. In moods of insobriety the results were quite otherwise. Great gobs of phlegm missed their target by inches, sometimes feet, each outburst of firing preceded by a noise of gyrating machinery as Bretherton cleared the depths of his throat and, as he put it, "fetched it up". The resulting decoration of the old Dickensian fireplace was singularly charming.

But with the onset of the racing season my nausea at all these things suddenly went beyond hatred. There is a condition of impotency in anger which, being inexpressible in either deed or language, is more frightful than action itself. It was becoming a case of "I rage, I melt, I burn"; I knew I couldn't last much longer; I knew that I was not only a bad reporter but would never be a good one. The poet in me, once as fresh and burgeoning as any spring blossom, had committed, or was about to commit, dark suicide.

Hereabouts, as if to make things worse, something else happened. A letter from Con told me that she was out of hospital and could we meet? Accordingly, I think on a Saturday afternoon, I went over to Kettering and we met where we had so often met and had so often made oblivious and passionate use of the First Class waiting-room. As we faced each other for the first time for several months I was assailed by a chill and inexplicable doubt; I felt that we were strangers. We walked out into the country, not talking much. At first the little we had to say to each other was normal, trivial, estranged too. Soon there came over me a further, even chillier feeling: that she had greatly changed. In vain I searched for some remnant of the warmth we had shared before her accident and before my own trial by boredom on the paper. My search merely yielded a stunning and unpalatable truth. Always inclined to be dominant and demanding, it was now clear that she was also unutterably spoilt. Long weeks of doting and devotion by nurses and doctors had covered her with an enamel of impossible, selfish aloofness. Almost all of what she had to say was of herself and nothing but herself and the distance at which it was said grew unhappier and greater as the afternoon went on.

The birth and growth of first love is a great wonder; the death of it is fearful; the premonition of its demise perhaps more fearful still. As I went home that day I must have experienced something of the feeling that a sick patient, petrified by the thought of a feared diagnosis of some malignancy being confirmed, at last has it confirmed. For my own part I knew that love was not merely in danger of being extinguished; it was already shrivelled. For some days I searched the territory of my own emotions trying to rationalize the whole affair as being the result of my own miseries with police courts, *Sporting Tissue in 'is Shirt* and the gobbing Bretherton. But in the end self-analysis had no such comforting solution to offer. It was a case of *Since There's No Help Come Let us Kiss and Part*, with all the nagging regret of that poem's final lines to bruise me further. With a melancholy that deepened to an inexplicably deeper loneliness I knew that it was all over.

I was now rapidly approaching a condition well expressed by H. G. Wells in his own *Autobiography*, a condition which in his case arose from the fact that he was indentured as a draper's apprentice (for which his mother, incredibly, had put down the munificent sum of fifty pounds) for a total period of four years, of which he had served only two. I was not so indentured, but the fact is that Wells, after two years, and I, after only two months, had reached precisely the same point. Wells, though frequently urged by his poor harassed mother to pray for help "in the right quarter" had nevertheless decided "that the drapery business was a dismal trap and I meant to get out of it". This he duly did and in later years he had this to say of it:

"I had reached a vital crisis of my life. I felt extraordinarily desperate and, faced with binding indentures and maternal remonstrances, I behaved very much like a hunted rabbit that turns at last and bites . . . I had discovered what were to be for me for some years the two guiding principles of my life. 'If you want something sufficiently, take it and damn the consequences . . . If life is not good enough for you, change it: never endure a way of life that is dull and dreary, because after all the worst thing that can happen to you, if you fight and go on fighting to get out, is defeat, and that is never certain until the end which is death and the end of everything'." It was rather after this fashion, if not in exactly such words, that I now felt strongly disposed to speak to Bretherton. As it turned out, it was Bretherton who spoke to me; but before that happened an incident occurred which seemed of no importance at the time, but the results of which were of singular value thirty years later.

On a dark, cold and dismal evening I had been given an assignment by Bretherton to go to Rushden Hall to interview the owners and occupants, Mr and Mrs Sartoris, on what pretext I cannot now remember. The present Hall at Rushden is of Elizabethan date; but an earlier mansion on the same site was said to have been erected by the renowned John of Gaunt, Duke of Lancaster, "which was under a grant from the King to this famed personage". The position of the house in modern times is extraordinarily incongruous: an oasis of trees and avenues, the chief of which is (unless a rumour of its recent demolition is correct) composed of sixty-three ancient Wych elms, surrounded on all sides by boot factories, nineteenth and twentieth century developments, with all the chapels, bakeries and fish shops I have already described, together with today's supermarkets and coffee bars. But on that dark frigid night when I went to keep my assignment it was rather like penetrating to the heart of a medieval stronghold deep in a silent wintry forest.

Two great wooden gates were the only means of entrance on the town side, within sight of the tall-spired church, whose first incumbent had been Thomas de Northampton in 1231. By the gates stood a small gate-keeper's lodge with leaded windows and after I had rung the big iron-handled bell-pull the gate-keeper let me in. It seemed, and probably was, all of a quarter of a mile to the house and there was nowhere a light to be seen. Finally a glimmer or two emerged from beyond the heavy avenue of trees and after I had rung another bell at the front door of the house a maid let me in. I have an impression that the name Sartoris is French and I have a vivid recollection that the Sartoris' were extremely courteous and charming to me. I have an equally vivid impression that the house was like a refrigerator. A huge log fire burned in an enormous open fireplace but the effect of this on the great frigidity of the atmosphere was that of a match being applied to the walls of an iceberg. The walls were of panelled oak which either time or wood-smoke, or both, had turned completely black. There seemed to be a wholly unnecessary number of doors in the large room where the Sartoris' greeted me and each was draped in a curtain of heavy wine-red velvet, rather as if in the hope of keeping further cold out or the relative warmth of the room in.

It has passed completely from my mind what I had

come to interview the Sartoris' about, or what they said to me. Two impressions, however, remain unfaded: first, my own incomparable nervousness which, further actuated by the cold, kept me constantly shivering; and secondly the strangest feeling that the shaping Divinity had actually sent me there for a purpose which then appeared to be totally obscure. All that I bore away with me into the freezing blackness of the winter night was, in fact, in no sense real; it was in some sense both haunting and prophetic.

In fact it was not to become real for another thirty years, when that same room became the setting for the first chapters of a novel of mine. But since one room, like one idea doesn't necessarily make a novel, it was opportune that somewhere about the same time I had had another experience, even briefer but just as singular in its importance. One morning, as I went to catch my morning train, a smart pony-drawn gig drew up at the station and out of it got a tallish, dark, proud, aloof young girl in a black cloak lined with scarlet. I had never seen her before and never saw her again. Such a vision was not, in fact, ever to be seen in that town and I surmised, rightly or wrongly, that she came from the Hall.

In the writing of novels there must necessarily be a fusion of negative and positive. In this case the cold, dismal, wintry Hall was the negative; the girl in the scarlet lined cloak, seen for two minutes, was the positive. In fusion, thirty years later, they became *Love for Lydia*.

Bretherton now took it upon himself to speak to me. One morning he arrived at the office about eleven o'clock, in unsober, parsonic mood. It became clear that he was about to deliver a lecture, perhaps even a sermon, for my benefit. Its tone of alcoholic piety was incredible to hear. He addressed me as from some pulpit aloft.

I had now been with him for several weeks and what had been achieved? Nothing; precisely and absolutely nothing. I was lazy. I lacked initiative. I dreamed. I declined to ferret. Beyond the windows of the office lay a world teeming with incident or potential incident, not to say excitement. Had I ever investigated it? Never. It was a fundamental principle of journalism that it was no use waiting for events to come to you. You had to go after events. This I had failed, and failed dismally, to do. "Everything comes to him who waits" was an adage of great falsity. On the contrary nothing came to him who waited. I had waited. Result, not unnaturally in Bretherton's opinion, nothing.

In parsonic alcoholic tones Bretherton urged me earnestly to take note that he was saying all these things not for the good of his own soul but for my own. My behaviour, he confessed, pained him greatly. His hopes of me had been high. It was now incumbent upon him to have to tell me that these hopes had been dashed; I was, in short, a failure. It was extremely doubtful if I should ever make a journalist. That some potential in me existed he had no doubt, but how many times, if ever, had it shown signs of becoming reality? Few, he declared dolefully, few, very, very few.

He aimed to spit into the fire and missed. A greenish glob of phlegm dripped from the surrounding fire-place. The remonstration piously went on. It contained, I remember, a section on Opportunity. Great indeed, Bretherton painfully reminded me, was my Opportunity. He himself was a journalist who had served on great newspapers. He had made his mark in London. He now gave the impression that fate or the gods or some other power had sent him into my life to offer me the Great Opportunity. In this direction he was only too ready to serve, even to sacrifice. That I had talents, far off and deeply latent though they might be, he did not doubt. But that I had made not the slightest perceptible use of them he did not doubt either. It was all sad, all very, very sad. At this point it would not have been at all surprising to have seen a welling of tears in Bretherton's eyes. Instead the sermon ended with a benediction. I was dismissed not only with Bretherton's blessing but with the earnest beseechment that I must pull myself together, try to do better and above all to seize the Great Opportunity. I accepted both blessing and beseechment in silence and Bretherton nipped over to *The Hind* for another whisky.

Bretherton was a fair example of the old journalistic alcoholic fraud. Shabby, even scruffy, the Great Opportunity long since lost in mists of alcohol, he was a figure at once distasteful, despicable and pathetic. In one of Shaw's plays there is a devastating portrait of a journalist who resembles, in fact, a human ferret dressed in seedy, greasy mackintosh: a kind of younger Bretherton before the rot finally sets in.

That morning I could cheerfully have swiped Bretherton: not physically, small and overweight though he was, but metaphorically and mentally. My rage at the piety of that lecture of his brought me, as I rode home in the train, to a pitch of impotency very near to tears. Of all human attributes the first and foremost I cannot stand is hypocrisy and that morning my cup of it was full.

Next morning I informed Bretherton, and then my father, that I had turned my back on the Great Opportunity. In all my life I have never been so relieved.

CHAPTER
ELEVEN

I was now once again at the cross-roads; and once again there was no visible sign-post or hand to guide me.

Again I mooched about, waiting for something to turn up. The horizon was empty. Out of the generosity of his heart my father had bought me a second-hand bicycle for thirty shillings. It was never quite in tolerable working order but on it I clanked and squeaked about the spring countryside, drinking in the joys I had missed in the dingy office of *The Northampton Chronicle*, where one afternoon an incomparable young vision had turned up with her father, the proprietor, to cast an appraising eye on the impossible office and myself, as if I had been an inmate in a debtors' prison. I have often wondered what that aloof, lovely creature thought of me, the office and its dreary Dickensian fireplace choked with ashes.

In between my rides into the countryside I went to the reading room of the Carnegie Library to study advertisements both in London and local papers. The shadow of the Great Depression was by this time not far ahead and already jobs were difficult, if not impossible, to find: so impossible that it was only a year or two later that I found myself standing, in common with about three and a half million others, in a queue for the dole.

But presently I came upon an advertisement that seemed to offer something, if not a great deal. *"Clerk wanted for warehouse; good references; apply own handwriting etc."* More in desperation than hope I applied. Some mornings later I received a letter favourable in that it was at least a summons for an interview. It was from the manager of a firm of leather and grindery factors housed at an address a mere stone's throw from the gateway beyond which the genesis of *Love for Lydia* had taken place a few weeks before.

Duly presenting myself to what had once been an old paint store owned by the father of a former school-friend of mine, I met Mr Smart, the manager. Mr Smart was kindly, considerate and perceptive. He appeared to be impressed by my appearance and my Third Class Honours. Two days later I got the job: salary one pound a week, double what I had been getting from Bretherton and the Great Opportunity.

I should explain here that boots and shoes are not merely made of leather. They require an infinity of accessories. Hessian, linings, thread in all colours, cords, cottons, eyelets, rivets, nails, sprigs, insoles, heels, back-straps, glue, wax and heaven knows what: all these, together with a few skins of kid — the capacity of the old paint shop was too cramped for any heavier grades of leather — we kept in the old two-floored warehouse, which actually stood at the foot of the garden of a dear and attentive old lady, a certain Mrs Fountain.

On my first morning at the warehouse I was greeted by a short, rather abrupt man who announced himself as

"'Emmings. I come to show you the ropes for a week or two."

The first of the ropes Mr Hemmings proceeded to show to me was the outside lavatory, which was kept continually locked against possible night intruders. "Got to keep this clean," Mr Hemmings said. "I do like a clean 'ole."

The necessity of keeping the lavatory impeccably clean having been duly noted I accompanied Mr Hemmings on a tour of the warehouse and its mysteries. I scarcely understood a thing. Downstairs stood great piles, in sheets, of what seemed to be grey cardboard, together with bags of grindery, sprigs, nails, rivets and so on, and sacks of powdered glue. Upstairs were the various threads, cottons, hessians and linings. There was also in one corner a tiny office built of varnished match-boarding, containing a desk, a telephone, a few files, a typewriter and a petty cash-box from which I could extract an occasional few shillings for stamps and so on. All these things, Mr Hemmings explained to me, were to be my responsibility.

For the next two weeks Mr Hemmings showed me, and showed me very adequately, the ropes. Among other things he taught me the only thing that I can still do in a professional manner with my hands: namely, packing parcels. Now and then Mr Smart appeared, took an appraising glance or two about the place to observe that all was in order, did *The Daily Express* cross-word puzzle and then disappeared on his commercial travels. His territory ranged from northward of the Nene Valley, where desecrated little villages such as Finedon,

Ringstead, Burton Latimer and Raunds all had their typical nineteenth-century shoe factories, to as far south as Wollaston and even Olney, William Cowper's town, over into Buckinghamshire. All these were small fry in comparison with the many factories of Rushden and Higham Ferrers combined where, as I have said, huge mushroom fortunes had been made in the years of the First World War.

After Mr Hemmings' eventual departure it did not take me long to assess that I held a position of unique and exceeding advantage to myself: I was alone practically all day and every day. A few orders having been executed, a few telephone calls answered, I found that I had little to do between eight-thirty in the morning and five-thirty in the evening. I at first took advantage of this to read voraciously. I devoured Conrad, Bennett, Wells, Galsworthy and Hardy; I gnawed into *Of Human Bondage*; I somehow discovered the American writers Joseph Hergesheimer, Edith Wharton, Willa Cather and James Branch Cabell; I grasped at *Madame Bovary* as at the fruit of a rare tree; I practically exhausted the contents of the shelves of the Carnegie Library, consuming in the process a mixed menu of May Sinclair, W. W. Jacobs, Tennyson Jesse, Perceval Gibbon, Stacy Aumonier, John Russell, Chesterton and a particular little gem, greatly formative in its influences on me, Hilaire Belloc's *Hills and the Sea*. I even kept a sort of diary, a record of the things I read, and soon its pages were fat to overflowing.

All this was far removed from what might have been my curriculum at Cambridge, but it must be remembered

160

that I was still only seventeen and that in any case Cambridge at that time would still have been some distance away. The direction of my voyage of literary discovery was now, come hell or high water, to be of my own choosing. I had no one to teach me navigation. It is true that I went back one afternoon to school for the purpose of hearing a lecture by De la Mare, an exercise in the way language might be used that I have not forgotten; (De la Mare took as his text the sentence *Won't you dine with me tonight?* and then with skill proceeded to demonstrate how, by the change of emphasis from word to word, the entire meaning of the sentence could be shifted half a dozen times) but this was all. Instead, the first of my own foragings began to yield unexpected fruit. One afternoon — it may well have been the one on which I had gone to listen to De la Mare — I was waiting for a train by the bookstall at Kettering Station when I spotted a large-paper remainder called *The Windmill*, an anthology of stories, essays and verse put out by the firm of William Heinemann, whose imprint the windmill was. I bought the book, I think for two shillings.

Much of its contents surprised and fascinated me. There were authors of whom I had never heard. Two in particular were Herbert Crackanthorpe, a name utterly unknown, I fancy, to the present generation, and Stephen Crane, who was represented by a story called *The Five White Mice*, a highly economical and vivid tale of a gambling joint which took its title from a ditty that went:

Oh! five white mice of chance,
Shirts of wool and corduroy pants,

161

> Gold and wine, women and sin
> All for you if you let me come in —
> Into the house of chance.

It was not, however, the ditty that impressed me so much. It was the way the story began:

Freddie was mixing a cocktail. His hand with the long spoon was whirling swiftly, and the ice in the glass hummed and rattled like a cheap watch. Over by the window, a gambler, a millionaire, a railway conductor, and the agent of a vast American syndicate were playing seven-up. Freddie surveyed them with the ironical glance of a man who is mixing a cocktail.

The vastly mature tone of this pictorial piece impressed me greatly. Whose was this new voice ? I had heard nothing like it before. A considerable number of years later I pointed out, in the *Modern Short Story*, that a short story can be likened to a horse-race; it is the beginning and end that count most and of these two it is probable that the beginning is of the greater importance. In this respect Crane's story went almost as well as that of *The Prodigal Son* in the Authorised Version, where in six words the author of that incomparable little story, consisting as it does of a mere 130 words or so, succeeds in introducing his three main characters. In a single brief paragraph Crane introduced five. Nor was this all. Crane was also making his words work overtime, not only bringing his characters to immediate and vivid life, but succinctly setting the atmosphere in which they were ready to move.

A new light now opened up for me. I thirsted for more

Crane and indefatigably set out on a hunt for him. The Carnegie Libraries offered nothing. I drew blanks at bookshops (only a little later I was to draw equal blanks when searching for Donne). I could find nothing in catalogues. How it finally came about that I succeeded in tracking down *The Open Boat* and *The Red Badge of Courage*, that most extraordinary epic of the American Civil War which had shot Crane into stardom in the 1890's, I cannot now remember, but eventually I did, later finding also *The Third Violet* and *Bowery Tales*. Later, when I mentioned my Crane enthusiasms to A. E. Coppard he reacted with no little scorn, declaring "Crane me no Cranes", perhaps not an altogether unexpectedly blind admission from a writer who had been unwise enough to take that most elephantine of bores, Henry James, as the chief of his models. For my part no charge of explosive could remove me from my ironclad admiration of a man who could start a story, *The Open Boat*, with the nine words *None of them knew the colour of the sky*. When you read a story beginning in that fashion you begin to revise very sharply your pre-conceived notions of the way a story can be written.

It is to Crane, therefore, that I really owe my first conscious hunger to begin writing stories, which I did when I was seventeen. Crane had also begun writing when very young but, as far as I was concerned, with this pregnant difference: unlike me but like the young Maupassant he had arrived on the literary scene fully equipped. He had nothing to learn. He never really knew how good he was. Just as Maupassant had amazed and shocked his established elders with the unparalleled maturity of *Boule de Suif*, so Crane had stunned the American and English literary world with *The Red Badge of Courage*, an epic of a war in which Crane had not, and could not possibly have, taken part. Its authority alone is dazzling enough; its realism cuts like a scalpel. Yet the book, after someone had declared that it outdid Zola, Tolstoy and Kipling in one breath, suffered at first a critical fate dismal in the extreme. All manner of excuses were offered for its rejection: it had no love story; it was too grim (this of what was then the bloodiest war in history); veterans of war found it insulting, unpatriotic, damned nonsense; others felt that it betrayed the memory of the slain; as to the author himself and his then revolutionary style "it was passionately urged that no decent youth should describe emotions in terms of colours, that his grammar was wildly mouldy." Nevertheless, thanks in no little part to "the blaze of English reviews", the book became stupendously successful and Crane found himself famous — fatally famous it would not be too much to say — by the time he was twenty-four.

The Red Badge of Courage is not a long book. Though packed with action, blood and the emotions of the starry-eyed young hero who goes to war in the expectation of glory and leaves it chastised by the white heat of disillusionment — emotions that certain horrified critics believed should not and could not be expressed in colour — it somehow conveys the impression of epic structure. As a comment on this it is interesting to note that *War and Peace*, Tolstoy's "endless panorama", annoyed Crane. "He could have done the whole business in one-

164

third of the time and made it just as wonderful. It goes on and on like Texas." Exactly. Not for the first time, nor the last I fear, had sheer length and size seduced readers into the mesmerised belief that they were in the sacred presence of greatness.

It was not only the painterly quality of Crane's prose that attracted me, nor the forceful insistence on describing emotions in colour, but also a sharp and dominant element of poetry. Though I can find in D. H. Lawrence's letters no mention whatever of Crane it seems to me that there is much in common with the early short stories of Lawrence and those of Crane. It is a well known fact that when a scientist unravels a problem of fearsomely intricate nature in one part of the world it is a fair bet that some other scientist, or scientists, are about to make a similar revelation in another (the discovery by William Harvey of the circulation of the blood is a celebrated example of this). When therefore I read in Lawrence's *Odour of Chrysanthemums* the passage

"The small locomotive, number 4, came clanking, stumbling down from Selston with seven full wagons. It appeared round the corner with loud threats of speed, but the colt that it startled from among the gorse, which still flickered indistinctly in the raw afternoon, out-distanced it in a canter," I can almost hear the echo of it in Crane's *"The battle lines writhed at times in the agony of a sea-creature on the sands. These tentacles flung and waved in the extreme excitement of pain,"* and I know also that I am in the presence of two men who, though oceans apart as far as terrestrial distances are concerned, have arrived at an identical point where they

165

have simultaneously discovered that writing is not merely done with hand and brain, but also with the eyes. Young as I was I recognised in Crane, and later in the earlier Lawrence, proof that words, as well as pigments, can also paint.

It was some months however, before I began to practice my apprentice hand at short stories. Poems I was still writing: poems that went, like unwanted strays, from editor to editor, bringing back, like faithful puppies, nothing but rejection slips between their teeth. Neither the remotest hint of an acceptance, nor an encouraging word, ever reached me.

In the autumn of my seventeenth year, however, I decided to write a novel. My system of getting the greater part of the warehouse work finished by about nine-thirty every morning having proved almost consistently successful I went off one evening and bought myself the thickest quarto writing pad, in pale blue, that I could find. I bought it in fact from a shop run by two elderly maiden sisters, one half of the shop being devoted to books, stationery, inks, pens and so on, the other to rather exclusive brands of chocolate, sugared almonds, toffees, marzipan and various sweetmeats such as crystallised violets, rose petals and those silver bullet-like balls that are used to decorate wedding and birthday cakes. For some reason the two ladies, both of whom wore those high-necked collars of lace that at once give an impression of stiffness, disapprobation and aristocracy, seemed to disapprove of me. Perhaps they had not unfounded suspicions that I found the young girl behind the stationery counter particularly attractive;

perhaps they were also suspicious and mystified that a youth of seventeen could possibly need so much writing-paper, even for writing letters — perhaps love-letters? — at one time.

I bore home that massive chunk of writing-paper with a feeling of rare and peculiar excitement in my heart: an emotion arising from a particular sort of anticipation that has since been repeated a thousand times. Talking only the other day to a celebrated painter I discovered that she too had shared, over and over again, the same anticipatory thrill: hers from a blank area of canvas, mine from a naked quarto of paper. What, eventually, is going to illuminate the canvas, what the paper? The question is still, for me, the most exciting one of a writer's life — out of, and by means of, the simplest materials, will come what? The mere fact of not knowing is over and over again responsible for a positive, impossible excitement.

Almost every morning that autumn and winter, after lighting the big coke-burning stove, called I think *The Tortoise* and not inappropriately, I settled down to write in the warehouse. Sometimes the telephone bell, a customer, a drayman from the railway goods yard interrupted, but progress was mostly undisturbed, peaceful and rapid. Though filling both sides of the paper I was not long in returning to the lace-collared ladies and their charming assistant for a fresh supply. As my novel grew so, it seemed, did the coolness of the ladies' disapproval. What *could* a young man possibly need with so much paper, and so often?

They did not know; and nor, in fact, did anyone else.

I wrote like a hermit. This is not to say that I cut myself off completely from the world of football, Chaplin's *Easy Street* and Griffith's *Birth of a Nation* at the cinema, or, when summer came round again, from cricket, tennis and much bicycling into the countryside. That hermit-like part of my existence was merely a first demonstration of the indisputable fact that creation, in art of any kind, is of necessity secret. The fusion between writer and paper, painter and canvas cannot, or should not be, shared. Such sharing was called by D. H. Lawrence, with complete aptitude, as I have already said, "the give away".

It is beyond all dispute, I now have to confess, that my hermit-like industry did not prevent my novel from being an untidy, verbose and appalling shambles. In Crane's words "like Texas it went on and on", and unhappily, I fear, to no purpose. When it was finished I sent it off, in MS, since I couldn't afford the cost of typing, to Edmund Kirby, who in reply permitted himself a few comments of such a guarded nature that I was disposed, with melancholy but justly, to submit to the verdict that I had spawned a shapeless, amateurish, useless monster. Indeed I had.

A certain buoyancy of character is something I have never lacked and with very little of any kind of protracted pain I buried the blue bundle of words away in a drawer, like a creature still-born. But the world being full of novels that are begun but never finished I had at least this singular piece of satisfaction to comfort me: bad as it might be, I had finished my novel, all 150,000 words of it; and this, since the act of writing is, like the act of love, primarily a physical affair, whatever emotions inspire it or it may engender later, was something of not inconsiderable importance. Having run one marathon, though in unspectacular time, I assured myself that I could attempt another.

The genesis of novels and stories, as Hardy once pointed out of *Tess*, often stems from the simplest, most fleeting of moments. A word, a glance, a face are, more often than not, enough; though not, of course, for the Texan-like acres of *War and Peace*. My next novel, which in fact was to be my first to be published, *The Two Sisters*, had its genesis after this simple fashion: it sprang simply from the sight of a candle, or lamp, burning in a window. I was much given to walking alone at this time, more especially at night, and it was on a stygian, moonless night, I rather fancy in January, that I found myself walking through the tiny hamlet of Farndish, in the neighbourhood of which the Romans indisputably delved for iron. Half way down the village street I passed a biggish, square stone house in one room of which the curtains were not drawn. A light burned inside. I stopped for a moment, stared through the window into a room of a strange and shadowy emptiness and was instantly gripped first by a haunting sense of melancholy and then by the indefinable notion that I had been there, in front of that lamp-lit window, before. I went home greatly troubled in imagination. A new genesis had begun.

The word imagination is here of no little importance. The business of writing fiction is an exercise in the art of telling lies. If the writer uses his art and craftsmanship to

169

their fullest extension he will not only succeed in making his readers believe that his lies are truth but that they are in fact truer than life itself. The writer without imagination, or the ability to invent, is not a writer of fiction at all. It is fidelity to imagination, therefore, not fidelity to observation, that is of supreme importance to the writer of fiction, whether it be in the form of the novel, the short story or the play. I have little use for so-called novels such as *Point Counter Point*, brilliant though they may be, which offer a sort of superior parlour guessing game designed to get the reader to spot the life-size originals of the characters involved; nor have I any more use for such a novel as that absurd and grossly overpraised piece of D. H. Lawrence's, *Women in Love*, which is not only the worst of all the bad novels he ever wrote but is almost beyond dispute the worst novel ever written by a writer of international reputation. The transposition from Bloomsbury of characters such as Lady Ottoline Morrell and Co to the hills and woodlands of Derbyshire, is a piece of incongruous lunacy, resulting in a novel that is like a bad patch-work quilt, part silk, part homespun, ending in nothing but a mess. Even before *Sons and Lovers* (a considerable number of the uninvented characters Lawrence used in the earlier novel *The White Peacock* are still alive in Nottinghamshire today) Lawrence had demonstrated that, brilliant in power of observation as he was and as the early short stories and poems indisputably demonstrate, he hadn't enough imagination to invent Mickey Mouse. As for inventing a new main character for each novel as it was written this was totally unnecessary; Lawrence himself was always there to oblige as the hero and did indeed oblige, over and over again and to a point of utter tedium, until the end.

It is true to say, of course, that a very great percentage of first novels are autobiographical; and perhaps inevitably. Twenty or thirty years of a writer's experiences, whether of love, family conflicts, quarrels, soul-searching, embracing or rejection of beliefs and creeds, may well forcefully cry out to be set down in that first precious essay. All, to the young writer, is of inflaming importance; all must go in. Not so with the second novel. Here arises the hard, gristly problem on which so many writers have broken their teeth. All has gone in; what now? Mere power of observation, however penetrative and brilliant, is now not enough. Unless power of imagination is there to stimulate a new and green insurgence of character, scene and conflict, a mere desert looms ahead. A process of telling lies, of distortion, of omission, of twisting, of conjuring, of deception — call it what you will — is now the one indisputable and imperative art that will make the desert blossom.

My purpose in mentioning all this is to make clear that *The Two Sisters* was a work solely of imagination: indeed it would not be untrue to say of wild imagination, the rampaging, highly-coloured, not always quite coherent imagination of youth trying to say something but not knowing quite what it wanted to say. The only solid piece of fabric in it was the lamp in the window of an otherwise dark house on a stygian night in January. This house I proceeded to people with two sisters, wholly different in character, a slightly unbalanced father who kept them half-imprisoned there, a young man from the outside world who comes as a bearer of love and liberation, and a servant: none of whom were based on living people I had met before. In short it was not a work of observation, but one of poetry. Nor was it a novel of chronicled realism, but one of essentials: what had been left out was more important than what had been left in. It did not in any degree follow the pattern of the autobiographical essay that was elsewhere described as "the easy plan, in which the author declaims that 'I am going to tell you all about myself and my friends, the characters and their families, and their neighbours, and their surroundings, and their past and their present and everything else just as I can think of it.'" In other words the writer who seeks to tell everything succeeds, all too often, in telling nothing. How many Victorian three-deckers ever said as much in one chapter as Crane said in *None of them knew the colour of the sky?*

Every word of The Two Sisters was written in the warehouse. I fear that I have perhaps slightly exaggerated in saying that I got down to the business of writing every morning: solely, perhaps, because those are the only mornings that meant anything or gave me pleasure. There was, of course, other work to do, but I can only say that I did it as rapidly as possible. I had letters to write, typing with one finger; a little simple bookkeeping to do; accounts to make up and bills to pay; orders to take and pack and despatch. Large, heavy drays, drawn by large heavy horses, arrived frequently from the station goods yard, bringing merchandise from

Manchester, Bradford, Birmingham, Scotland and various parts, so that I was flung into the fierce physical activity of unloading it all and stowing it away. Sometimes an urgent call from a factory made it essential for me to set off on a half-running errand with sack barrow, a parcel or a quarter hundredweight sack of nails on my shoulder. In winter the little warehouse became an icebox, in summer a stifling oven.

Thirsty or chilled, I was constantly being cosseted by the motherly attentions of Mrs Fountain, the lady next door. Mrs Fountain had an incurable habit of "popping in". At eleven o'clock in the morning she would "pop in" with bread and cheese or biscuits and tea; in the afternoon she again "popped in" with tea, cake and buttered toast. She fussed over me; she liked a little gossip. In her garden she had apple and pear trees and on the warehouse wall a plum; in their season she brought me the fruits of these too. I have some idea that she thought I was overworked, which in one sense was true, in another not. The warehouse work, for which after one year my wage rose to the princely heights of thirty shillings a week, was a mere necessity; it was the business of writing *The Two Sisters*, in secret and mostly at break-neck speed, and then of hiding the MS away into a disused drawer at night, that provided the overworking and in due course that lean and hungry look which Mrs Fountain and her "poppings-in" sought to do something to comfort.

I suppose I worked on *The Two Sisters* for a year; it is hard to remember. Until a short time ago I had long been under the impression that I wrote two versions of it; but then, searching among some early papers, I discovered a third, or part of a third. These facts provide the key to something which has been stubbornly part of my character and practice as a writer ever since: I was, and still am, frigidly and restlessly self-critical. "I have destroyed hundreds of poems," wrote Rupert Brooke, "for my soul's sake." I can say with equal truth that I have destroyed scores of poems, several plays, many short stories and three novels not for my soul's sake but simply because the disciplinarian in me thought they were no damn good.

But at last there was finished a version of *The Two Sisters* with which I was evidently not altogether displeased. Furious and blind though the urgencies of its creation had been (I once wrote no less than 12,000 words of it, among the leather, linen and thread, in one day.) I evidently felt, at last, that I had produced a work that was not only coherent but at least measurable by the standards — the standards of a very youthful nineteen, it must be remembered — I had set myself. Still no one but myself knew of its existence, but now, thanks to the munificence of my salary, I could at least afford to get it typed.

Thus, in the early months of 1925, it started on its first excursion to the outside world; while I, supremely confident that the hunger of one publisher would be enough to consume it in the matter of a day or two, a week at the outside, unexpectedly set out on another.

CHAPTER
TWELVE

It is well to be truthful and succinct about this event. Nowadays, when we are near-suffocated by trade-unionese, councilese and Americanese, the new extensions of stodge-pudding language that have joined Johnsonese, journalese and politicalese, it would no doubt be said that I became redundant. I prefer the old way: I was unexpectedly sacked.

Whether my secret predilection to give most of my time to writing had been suddenly discovered or long-suspected and tolerated meanwhile for lack of proof I shall never know. One day I was simply told that my services at the warehouse were no longer required. It was a fearful blow; in vain I protested. Quite apart from the loss of wages, which had now risen to positively royal heights at two pounds a week, there was also a crushing loss of pride. I actually felt that I had done some sort of wrong, a notion that may well have also occurred to my employers, who might reasonably have felt that the business of trading in the accessories necessary to shoe-making, though including many odd and diverse things, did not include the writing of novels. I now feel some sympathy for them on that score.

I was, anyway, suddenly out on the street. The cloud

of the Great Depression was only a short distance away; already unemployment was rising everywhere; a system known as three on and three off (i.e. three days of work and three of dole) was already operating in the majority of factories; many firms were closing down; in less than ten years the huge golden balloon of the war-time boom had collapsed to the size and appearance of a pig's bladder blown up by boys (as we often used to do) who had otherwise no ball to play football with in those ash-strewn back-alleys we called "jitties". A new, ungay company of strolling players had already appeared on the streets, many of them short of a finger or two, a hand, an eye or even a leg, hawking wares such as boot-laces, scrubbing-brushes, soap, polishes and so on. I observed them not with pity but with anger: so much so that whenever I read of the play *Look Back in Anger* I am inclined to laugh with brittle mockery. Neither Mr Osborne nor those who unwisely over-praised his piece or failed to recognise that its real title should have been *Look Back in Self-Pity* can have had the remotest notion what the causes of anger can be. They should have seen the decent, piteous peep-show of the mid-twenties, in which I was half-spectator, half-player, an almost ferocious predecessor of Mr Osborne's angry young man by a quarter of a century and with truer, more bitter cause.

Nevertheless a certain natural buoyancy of temperament prevented my being too pessimistic about my personal affairs. It was true that I was once again at the cross-roads, not knowing which way to turn and having no guidance on the subject anyway, but at least I now had the novel. I had great hopes of the novel. I think I sent it first to William Heinemann, perhaps because they were the publishers of Crane and Maugham; then to Chatto & Windus, Constable, Dent, Chapman & Hall, Allen & Unwin, Harrap and more. From all these it duly came back. (Perhaps it was just as well that I didn't know at this time of the thirteen years' wandering of Joyce's *Dubliners* before it found a publisher: as incredible a piece of readership blindness as ever tarnished the publishing world.) And from all except two it came back with no syllable of comment. The exceptions were Dent, with whom I had a not unhopeful correspondence, more on my own potentialities as a writer, I think, than on the virtues of the book itself; and Chapman & Hall, of whom at that time the head was Arthur Waugh, father of Evelyn and Alec. Some considerable correspondence ensured as a result of their interest in the book and Waugh senior is said to have remarked "this young man has something to say". The interest expressed in this remark led in fact to my going to London, I think twice, to climb the stairs once trodden by Meredith, that figure so greatly revered at the turn of the century who is now utterly put away in moth-balls, to discuss the merits of *The Two Sisters* with a lady whose name now escapes me but who was most generous in both intelligence and kindness. It began to appear, soon, that the book might be accepted; I was buoyed up with miraculous hopes. These were finally dashed by the verdict of Alec, who decided that, after all, the book was not for Chapman & Hall.

So on its journeyings from publisher to publisher went

the novel again. It is also just as well that I didn't know that at about the same time Hemingway had sent his famous and excellent story *Fifty Grand* to every editor in America before its merits were finally observed by that acutest of editors, Ellery Sedgewick, of *The Atlantic Monthly*. Sedgewick had a sharp nose for talent and it was he, on quite another plane, who one day walked into the London offices of The British Weekly, asked if there was anything new to read and was told that the only MS of consequence, and not much consequence at that, was a little piece called, *Good-bye, Mr Chips*. Quick as a whippet after a hare, Sedgewick spotted the story's vast potentiality for success among an American public always ready to shed an honest tear or two, and the fame of James Hilton, whose later Hawthornden Prize-winning novel *Lost Horizon* actually and incredibly begins with that clanking cliché "cigars were burning low", was suddenly assured.

But as yet I had no such good fortune and meanwhile funds, never very high, were running very low. From the first moment of unemployment a staunch and mountainous pride had prevented me going on the dole. But soon the arguments for this, for me, most repugnant of steps became irrefutable. I had, after all, paid my insurance stamps and insurance against times of need was what such payments were for. We were not now, I was told, back in the days of Dickens; it was no longer a question of "going on the parish"; it was something to which I was fairly and honourably entitled.

With hate in my heart, I gave in, joining the dole queue every Friday ("signing on", I think they called it) at some small disused chapel in one of those precariously steep streets of which Rushden is full, and duly drew my dole, the sum of one pound. In the company of a rambling, coughing, shambling queue I could never quite rid myself of a sense of shame and I invariably scurried away without speaking to a soul, very often slipping out for a solitary tramp into the countryside in order to clear my lungs of those sounds of hauking, spitting and coughing which were so much part of the melancholy chorus of those days before tuberculosis had been conquered. If ever there was money that was hateful to me it was that I drew on those wintry Friday mornings in the year 1925.

All this time I was reading with my usual voracious appetite, always extending its range. During the previous August I had gone off with my parents for a week, perhaps two weeks, to Bournemouth, and had discovered in particular one of several bookshops there. The man I was after now — and I cannot now remember what first inspired it — was Turgenev. It appeared, however, that he, like Crane and Donne (the great revival of interest in Donne was still a few years ahead) was undiscoverable. But after much diligent search I at last tracked him down, finding him in a bookshop where the early Constance Garnett translations, in their plain khaki covers, were securely shut away in glass-doored cases, as if long unwanted and forgotten. I think I first bought *A Sportsman's Sketches*, at two shillings a time, in the edition of 1895. They were at once, for me, a source of great delight and influence; neither the English novel nor the English short story contained anything so poetical or so exquisitely full of the breath of summer mornings or the atmosphere of Russian birch forests clearing slowly from the cover of autumnal mists to the rising warmth of sun. Hemingway, for all his alleged toughness as a writer, was also so rejoiced and influenced and if you listen carefully you can, I think, hear the voice of Turgenev in the following lines:

"The breeze was coming up and we could hear it in the high branches. It was cool in the shade, but if you stirred in the sun, or as the sun shifted the shadow while you read so that any part of you was out of the shadow, the sun was heavy ... I could smell the heat of the day coming, the drying up of the dew, the heat on the leaves, and the heaviness of the sun over the stream."

Until I later read Hudson and Edward Thomas I discovered nothing in English prose to equal the exquisite nature of those sketches of Turgenev written so long ago. My next step, not unnaturally, was Tchechov. Young as I was, it didn't take me long to assess the vast potentialities of a writer of stories who so often says more by what he leaves out than by what he leaves in. Tchechov was followed by Maupassant, Gorki, Flaubert, Bierce and a considerable company of others whose main passion was, as mine was now, the short story. Galsworthy and Bennett, also in turn supposedly influenced by Turgenev, I had by now partially exhausted. My nose, for ever sniffing after new names, even found Knut Hamsun's *Hunger*, a book which Henry Miller still confesses he finds a great one.

Driven by these innumerable new influences I was now, undaunted by the fruitless journeyings of *The Two*

180

Sisters, writing a good many short stories. One autumn day it happened that I was playing football in Bedford. After the match the whole team repaired to a restaurant called *The Silver Grill*, where my guess is that, famished after the heat of the game, we drank much tea and ate fish-and-chips. A small harassed waitress, run off her feet by having to serve an entire football team and several spectators, scurried hither and thither with tea-pots, dishes of fried plaice and mounds of bread-and-butter, now and then pausing breathlessly at a serving hatch to snatch up a speaking tube and send her orders to the kitchen downstairs. I watched her, fascinated not because she was pretty, which she was not, but because already my imagination, like Hardy's with *Tess* and my own with the lamp in the window, was excitedly beginning to weave a pattern of lies about her.

The next morning I sat down and put that little waitress on paper in a very short story called *The Flame*. More than forty years later it is still a story of which I am not ashamed and which in fact was one of the stories in my first volume of stories, *Day's End*. But it too went off unsuccessfully on its wanderings: finding, like Joyce's *Dubliners*, no sponsors, a fact perhaps not surprising in that it was looking for one in a world where stories still had to have plots or to conform to rigid house-rules designed to satisfy the specific appetites of specific readers. My little harassed waitress in *The Flame* didn't need a plot; nor had I, then or later, any need for either plots or patterns imposed by others.

But, happily, changes were coming.

CHAPTER
THIRTEEN

It would be wrong to suppose that the world of the nineteen-twenties was entirely one of bitterness. On the contrary much of it was gay: strenuously, defiantly, noisily, swaggeringly, falsely gay. The young of all classes were in protest and revolt against their elders, but their protestations took on a form very different from those of the young of the present day. Where the young now march about cities with battle cries of violence and angry waving of banners, staging sit-ins, love-ins and so on, drinking much and trading much, apparently, in drugs, the young of the twenties merely rode, if they could afford it, in fast sports cars, made a great whoopee on Boat Race nights and wore clothes thought to be just as outrageous and revolutionary as the Carnaby Street patterns, often flowered and tattered, of today.

In a working-class town, however, the form of protest was a far milder form and the cause of it invariably the same: money or the lack of it. A few of the progeny of boot manufacturers made rapidly rich during the war could afford fast smart sports cars, but most of the rest of us were lucky to have push-bikes. There were still few buses and a lot of people still walked a great deal. If you went on holiday to the seaside in August, as most people did (still for the one precious statutory week), you did so in trains crowded to the point of suffocation and subsequently lived in digs for a couple of pounds or less a week. Of social life (I speak of the world of cocktail parties and so on) artistic and musical life, there was practically none. When H. G. Wells wrote "in this world of gramophones, pianolas and the radio, it is worth noting that at the age of thirteen I had heard no music at all except an occasional brass band, the not very good music of hymn singing and organ voluntaries in Bromley church" he might well have been talking of my own world of the twenties, a world so remote from discotheques, television and millionaire singing groups as to make the earlier world of tennis, tea on the lawn, fairs and boxing booths, shop-outings in charabancs, chapel social evenings and parades of Friendly Societies with *their* banners proudly borne aloft at Sunday School Treats, seem both ridiculous and naïve. Indeed in all probability it was; but there were compensations.

For example we danced. We danced, indeed, a great deal. Moreover dancing was cheap. If my memory serves me correctly the price of admission to most dances was one-and-six (refreshments excluded) though on occasion we permitted ourselves the luxury of some dashing affair at three-and-six. Of really special affairs at half-a-guinea (so priced in order to keep out the riff-raff) and at which the girls wore long dresses and the men, of forced necessity, dinner-jackets, we knew, and could know, nothing. Our own affairs were confined to the Parish Hall, a local Institute of some kind, the Co-op Hall or, occasionally, to some village hall ten or a dozen miles out in the country, for which we had perforce either to hire some ancient and shaky private bus or, as is described in *Love for Lydia*, some equally ancient limousine taxi.

Most of us drank little or hardly at all; few of us could afford to do so. When the time came for refreshments we dashed with gallantry to fetch tea or coffee, jellies, cakes, sandwiches and sausage rolls for the ladies of our choice. How any of them managed to be of our choice is a problem that constantly defeats me. Rarely can women's dresses have been more hideous than they were in the twenties, never less seductive. The girl of the day was presented to you as a sort of line prop, straight, bosomless, with a skirt so short and tight that she invariably also appeared knock-kneed. To this ever-fascinating gear was added a cloche hat, which resembled more than anything else a chamber-pot without a handle, and a long row of beads or pearls. Where a girl was more generously gifted in the region of the bust she wore stays that gave the impression of being made of iron and since her hair was almost always Eton-cropped you got the further disturbing impression that Nature, caught half-way in the dilemma of whether to create a male or a female, had finally come up with a creature composite of both.

But line-props, chamber-pot hats, Eton-crops or what you will, we nevertheless fell for these young creatures as if they were sculptured like the Venus de Milo or the milky mountain peaks of flesh now displayed as a matter of course in such magazines as *Playboy*. I suppose that the world of straight short dresses (today's mini-skirt is

184

in a class wholly different), cloche hats and long ropes of pearls now appears as ludicrous to the women of today (at the present moment I observe that the latest Parisian fashion designers are about to compel or persuade women to go about as near as possible in a condition known, I believe, as "starkers") as the hour-glass figures of the years of my extreme childhood. But we, the men, didn't think so. We saw, we chased and, if we didn't always conquer, we fell. Our own great moments came in summertime, with an affair that I suppose must now be considered to be as ridiculous as the cloche hat: namely the Flannel Dance. Arrayed like young peacocks, we strutted forth in coats of many colours. My own blazer was striped in black-and-scarlet; others out-flashed it in purple-white-and-green; some were white edged with blue and emblazoned with escutcheons of school or club. Thus arrayed, we clomped around, prodigiously sweating to fox-trots, quicksteps and subsequently to the gymnastic gyrations of the Charleston and the Black Bottom, joyous to the music of saxophones, *Valencia* and *Ain't She Sweet?*

Envious as women always are, girls who could not perform these newest of movements sat out, huddled together like sour, drab butterflies. At dances such as these there was no such nonsense as the elegant little appointment card with its pencil attached by a silken cord in which a girl booked her engagements for the evening. We, on the contrary, rode in like young gladiators in competition for whatever creature had excited our fancy. Our rewards were twofold: long seasons of chilliness from those with whom we had neglected to dance and the precious reward of seeing home the girl with whom the better part of the evening had been fused. *Last Dance, Please*, was a call as challenging as any ordering you to get on your marks for the 100 metres in the Olympic Games.

It is strange now to think that though so many of my evenings (except, of course, in Lent) were so spent in such abandoned and superficial gaiety, my days were almost utterly solitary. If I were not working on stories of my own, I was not only reading avidly of Conrad, Turgenev, Tchechov, Maupassant, Crane and many others, but often doing exercises in deliberate imitation of their styles, probing and dissecting them in order to discover how, in their various and masterly ways, they achieved their effects. In this single-minded pursuit I was not at all unlike a certain celebrated golfer who, day after day, travelled a practice course armed with buckets of golf balls which he proceeded hour after hour to putt and putt and putt and putt, until at last perfection and championships had been achieved.

But now, somewhere about this time, there appeared, accidentally as a result of the world of dancing, another writer, totally unexpected; and another person, totally unexpected too and a great deal more important.

On the edge of the town, to the south, stood an extremely old farmhouse. Built of stone, with a stone-walled garden, it still reminds me of many old manorial gardens, half in decay, that you see in almost every part of France. To one side of it ran a brook, over which hung lines of large horse-chestnuts. At the back of the farmhouse were the usual cow-barns, stalls, stack-yards, hen-runs and pig-sties. Inside, the rooms were large and rambling. The kitchen had that warm, half-buttery, half-milky smell in which was also mingled the odour of cows and cow manure. There was also about the entire house an ancient and church-like smell, strong with wood-smoke and dampness.

The farmer and his wife were upright, God-fearing, hard-working, pleasant, flaxen-haired, non-conformist and productive. They had a family equally divided into three sons and three daughters: all different in character, temperament and looks. No house could have been more English, more rural or more like a survival from Thomas Hardy or my own grandfather's boyhood. The father, in his extreme uprightness, was rather quiet: a good-looking man of typical yeoman aspect. In the mother I always suspected there lurked a streak of repressed gaiety accompanied by another of wisdom: a wisdom alive enough to allow her three daughters to have, from time to time, a party.

To one of these parties — I think it may well have been a birthday party — I was invited; why, I don't quite know, but I have a strong suspicion that various hands were at work behind the scenes. I knew hardly anyone else who had been invited except the daughters of the house and the pleasant little girl who served in the shop, among the silver balls and crystallised violets, where I had bought my first chunk of writing-paper for my first novel. "I wish I could set down with certainty," says H. G. Wells, "all the main facts of this phase of my adolescence"; and so do I. But much of my youthful development resembles a picture that needs cleaning; dust and varnish have clouded a good deal of it; a general outline remains but much detail lies hidden or half-hidden under the yellow coating of time. But this much is certain: as with artistic and musical life, so it was with literature. I had not a soul in all the town to whom I could talk. Harry Byrom had already gone to pursue his scholastic way at King's College, London, and I saw him only between terms. I had had, it is true, a brief friendship with a schoolmistress who belonged, or felt she belonged, to a slightly upper middle-class and with her I had been able to share, for an unpassionate interval, some of my new-found enthusiasm for, among other things, Donne. Her father manufactured mineral waters. Some idea of his attitude to music — we never spoke of literature — may be gathered from the fact that he was apt to declare, as he unwillingly listened to Chopin or Schubert on the radio, that all modern pianists played with one finger. Her mother was rather precious and came, I rather think she felt, from a Good Family, thus suspecting that if her daughter ever married me it would be rather Beneath Her Station. Once, when the daughter was convalescing from some illness, I went and sat and read to them, the mother being the chaperone, choosing of all authors Donne and of all poems *I wonder by my troth what thou and I did till we loved*. I might well have wondered, since love we never did.

But the picture of that winter night of the party at the farmhouse needs little cleaning. The varnish of time has certainly obscured many of the faces that were there, but

188

I still see clearly the big farm kitchen, the huge low-ceilinged sitting-room, the girls in their typical nineteen-twenty dresses and the piles of home-made cakes, tarts, sandwiches, jellies, cheeses and sausage rolls. I can still smell the soft milkiness of the kitchen, the whiff of frigid cow-pungent winter air as the back door was opened and the wood-smoke of the farmhouse fires. As the evening went on we ate, drank — not a single thimble of alcohol of any kind, naturally — danced, played games, gossiped and flirted.

We danced, I suppose, to a gramophone. The games were simple: mostly, I think, charades. But from time to time there was much running up and down the bare ancient oak stairs, phases of hide-and-seek and the usual hilarity, accompanied by shrieking, as if seductions of some sort were taking place in the upper darkness. For my own part I remember getting tired of dancing, exchanging shallow gossip and generally running around. At last, I suppose somewhere towards midnight, I found myself sitting on the half-dark stairs with a girl I had never met before: fair-haired, blue-eyed, rather petite and barely seventeen.

I have always fancied myself to be rather quickwitted but she, it turned out, was just as quick. Though she was in fact a stranger to me I got the impression that I had in fact met her before. The truth is that I somehow mixed her up with someone else. This led to a certain confusion, further leading to light banter, in the conversation.

I asked her name.

"Marjorie," she told me. "But most people call me Madge."

I told her my name.

"I know," she said.

Soon after this, since it was only a day or two beyond Valentine's Day, I teasingly hinted that she must have received a heap of Valentines. By so doing I opened up a mystery. There was a certain special Valentine she could not account for. She didn't suppose that I could? With a growing sense of mischief I hinted that it wasn't beyond the bounds of possibility. With excitement and curiosity she begged to know who had sent it, while I, with the sense of mischief growing all the time, succeeded merely in making the mystery grow darker and darker, more and more excited. Without my ever having uttered a word to confirm it, it was clear before midnight that I was the Valentine's sender. I had in fact never sent a Valentine to a girl in my life but that night it was an unsent Valentine — unsent by me, that is — that introduced me to the affections of the girl I was eventually to marry. To this day she doesn't know the sender of that Valentine, except that she still strongly suspects me, and nor do I. The entire affair remains a classic example of the fact that if you tell the truth people rarely believe you; whereas if you tell lies, or hints of lies, they nearly always do.

We kissed in the protective darkness of the stairs, kissed again on the way home and finally on the porch of her house. Thereafter we began to meet very often and go out together. The thing that struck me at once was that she seemed far older than her years: a fact not

altogether surprising since she had lost her father and several other members of the family during the war and had rather been pushed, since then, from pillar to post, having to fend for herself a good deal. Her life and mine could hardly have been more different, although we lived only a street away from each other, had played the same street games and shared a number of friends. She showed an amazed disbelief in the fact that I wanted to be a writer and a still further disbelief that, having been blessed with a little higher education, I was still unemployed. She herself had attended that same National School where my father had worked out his tricks in the late nineteenth century, a building that had changed little, if at all, in the intervening years. By a painful coincidence its headmaster at the time of her attendance was none other than Harry Byrom's uncle, a rigid disciplinarian of the old school for whom she had little respect and less affection. She was not only a girl of immense popularity in the school itself but a girl, even at that early age, of great spirit: so much so that one day during the war she had seen her brother subjected to such a blatant beating in open class that she had instantly fled from the school to home, there to collect a soldier uncle, conveniently home on leave. Fresh from the blood-stained fields of France, powerful in body, artillery spurs jangling, the soldier uncle proceeded to wage with the headmaster a battle of which the issue was, I understand, never remotely in doubt.

When I say that we met and walked out together I mean walking in the same sense as I had walked, as a boy, with my father. Indefatigably we walked and walked and walked: very often for long distances on winter nights, when the blackness of remote country roads was often so intense that I am not ashamed to say that I was frightened, and when at last we saw, with great relief, rows of green-yellow lights winking out for miles across the wide river valley. We also had bikes and on these we could go farther afield: often on Saturdays to Bedford, that rather enervating town that with its pleasant promenade by the Ouse reminds me more than a little of certain towns on the river banks of Central France. In Bedford, in those days so much the haven of retired Army gentlemen who had seen service in India, Singapore and so on, there was a bookshop and a good bookshop at that. With not more than a shilling or two in my pocket I spent hour after hour in that bookshop and its fussy but well-stocked second-hand department, picking up precious items for my still small but growing library. Blessed bookshop, Hockliffe's.

But we went, also, to the remoter stretches of the Ouse, to its lovely serpentine course where the names of the villages are composed of consonants so softly ethereal that you feel you must whisper them. Here we discovered long, unpeopled, overgrown stretches of water, often of backwaters, where Monet might have painted his water-lilies. Here the big white flowers were as crowded on the water as the fish, mostly roach I fancy, that lay in shoals under the big leaning willows and poplars that shaded the backwaters on hot summer afternoons. Gigantic hemlocks brooded in the shadows like the ears of green elephants. Willow-herb and meadowsweet and yellow mimulus and purple loosestrife lined the river banks. Of sounds you only heard, sometimes for hours on end, the turning, a whisper too, of poplar leaves, the plop of a rising fish, the gentle dive of a water-vole, a breath of wind lightly brushing the stiff tall swords of reeds.

Armed with kettle, frying pan, eggs, bacon, sausages, bread, cheese, fruit and tea, we picknicked here over and over again, I finding wood for the fire, Madge doing the cooking. Young appetites staunched, bodies replete, we then lay in the sun, locked in long ecstatic embraces, half asleep. A voice at last of some cow-man bringing his cattle back to the meadows after milking-time would eventually remind us that the afternoon had dreamed itself away. Then we made tea again, fed the appetites of youth yet once more with cakes, buttered scones and tins of fruit. Sometimes in the business of washing up Madge would take off her shoes and stockings and dabble her feet and legs — the best legs in town, as my friends often and rightly reminded me — in some more shallow patch of water among the reeds. Presently cows and cow-man were silent again and we found ourselves embalmed in a final hour or so of utter peacefulness, in an abandoned world in which an occasional kingfisher broke like a blue and copper firework from shadow to sunlight and a pair of swans with a family of following cygnets steered a course of matchless grace through the water-lilies and the long combed green hair of under-water weeds.

Nearer home, within walking distance, I had discovered a small wood where dark purple violets grew so thick on the floor that you almost felt you had to take off your shoes and stockings before you picked your

way among them. They were followed later, in midsummer, by crowds of butterfly orchids: strange, cream-green stalks of a Chinese-like delicacy, a sort of floating ghostliness in the petals and a fragrance so exquisite and strong that when we took them home indoors, the heavy exotic breath of them was more overpowering than that of lilies. A little farther afield I discovered, one late April afternoon, another wood, this time rich with primroses and that rarity of the primula family, oxlips. It was very quiet in the warm broken sunlight and suddenly I found I was not alone. In a hollow walled by exposed old tree-roots of oak and hazel I had come upon a whole family of dancing, prancing little foxes ("give us the little foxes, that eat our vines, for our vines have tender grapes" — it would seem, I am told, that the little foxes, in France and elsewhere, still eat the tender grapes), a sight so enchanting in its mischievous grace that the following day I took Madge back to the wood to see them. To my great delight they were there again and in absolute silence we lay, half-hidden by hazel boughs, and watched them, gambolling and fooling and chasing each other in their first exercises of growing up, so that once again we were locked in a world a million miles from the stink and noise of factories, leather and machines and Monday morning fires of leather-bits in which we had both been born. I don't think, unless memory one day completely fails us through utter senility, that we shall either of us ever forget that dancing ballet of the little foxes among the sheets of primroses and oxlips; nor do I think that either of us, from that moment, ever doubted that that world of factories, leather, chapels and factory hooters was a world we somehow had to escape from.

Some time not long after this I went home with Madge to discover, strangely enough, in her mother's modest front parlour, a writer and a book both quite new to me. How Henry Lawson's *While the Billy Boils* ever found its way into that room I have not the remotest idea; but as soon as I opened the book and started casting an eye over its fifty and more stories and sketches of Australian life in the latter part of the nineteenth century I was acutely aware that here was a voice to which I had to listen. I suppose that the fact of my having been brought up in a working-class family, in a working-class town, in a working-class school and with no other friends than those among working-class people might well have given me a sense of resentment against democracy and the vernacular, at least as far as literature was concerned. On the contrary: it was the strong and vivid appeal of the vernacular in such stories as *Maggie* and *George's Mother* that had done much to attract me to Crane and which now in turn attracted me to Lawson.

Lawson's territory was mostly the Australian "road, the bush, the track, the shearer, the 'selector', the pub, the wharf, the river and the street": a world as remote from that of Henry James as the conversation pieces of the eighteenth century are from the prostitutes of Lautrec. Lawson had written most of his pieces for the famed *Sydney Bulletin*, but others had appeared in the *Sydney Worker*, *Sydney Truth*, the *Brisbane Boomerang*, and various New Zealand periodicals. He had also written poetry, but a poetry of such badness, "of rattling humour and sentimentality", that it has been likened to "a voice speaking to you through a bad telephone". Lawson was not a "literary" writer; his matter is of more importance than his manner, which is much inclined to be rough, crude and tough. He is less of a literary man than a reporter and it is worth noting that Crane had been warned, in his turn, not to mix reporting with his writing. Perhaps Lawson may best be described as a "realist-humorist", and it is certain that *Stiffner and Jim (Thirdly Bill)* is worthy to stand among the most hilariously funny stories ever written. But note, too, the rapid sketch-like quality of the style, colloquial, pictorial, snappy, as vivid in its effect as a Phil May drawing:

"We were tramping down in Canterbury, Maoriland, at the time, swagging it — me and Bill — looking for work on the new railway line. Well, one afternoon, after a long hot tramp, we comes to Stiffner's Hotel — between Christchurch and that other place — I forget the name of it — with throats on us like sunstruck bones, and not the price of a stick of tobacco."

No poet? How often it is — take good note here of "sunstruck bones" — that the poet finds his expression in prose. But Lawson, besides being colloquially funny ("You know one or two of these mugs. Bite one of their ears"), could also be sad. *The Union Buries its Dead* is almost offhand in its sadness but is saved from cynicism by a singular perfection of realism and truth, as in the description of the burial — "the fall of lumps of clay on a stranger's coffin doesn't sound any different from the fall of the same things on an ordinary wooden box." Let the shabby modern purveyors of four-letter words, many of them women, try their hands at doing better than that; if ever a sentence had a melancholy, dying fall it is that simple one of Lawson's. Yet of even greater sadness is *The Drover's Wife*, a mere sketch, not a story, of a drover's wife living a life of lacerating loneliness, "in a landscape of the everlasting, maddening sameness of the stunted trees", as she waits for a husband to return from the long droving spell up-country: a piece that caused at least one critic to say of its significance in two short pages that "even Tolstoy has never done better".

But curiously enough, much though I admired and still admire Lawson, he did not influence me as Crane, Bierce and even O. Henry had done. I rate style as high as matter; and at this particular period of my life I rated style, if anything, the higher of the two. If I had not very much to say of great profundity at the age of twenty I was determined that when at last my literary voice, so to speak, was properly broken, I should at least be in some command of the manner of saying what I had to say. I wanted words to be my servants, not my masters.

CHAPTER
FOURTEEN

I think if you had asked my grandfather what he most
wanted me to be he would have said "A Member of
Parliament". If you had put the same question to my
father he would most probably have replied "A minister
of the Church". Both, happily, were doomed to disappointment; and of the two my father's was undoubtedly the greater.

My father's position may be likened to that of a
diligent and dedicated farmer who had tilled his earth
industriously and sown his corn with care, only to
observe coming up, in due course, a crop of tares. I was
the tares.

The good sound corn that had been sown Sunday after
Sunday on my dutiful trottings off to Chapel, Sunday
School, Prayer Meeting and Bible Class had at last
brought forth exactly the opposite of the crop intended.
It could not even be argued that some seed had fallen on
stony ground, since the ground too had been prepared
and nurtured to a condition exactly right for receiving it.
In brief I suddenly and dynamically revolted. In vain my
father pointed out that several of my school-friends were
"to enter the Ministry". He may also have taken the
problem of my violent recalcitrance, as H. G. Wells'

mother did, to the "Heavenly Father, who remained, as ever, speechlessly enigmatical". I do not know; but it is to his eternal credit that he offered no show of violent or even mild remonstrance on my unforeseen backsliding; we had neither argument nor quarrel on the matter. Suddenly I no longer went to Chapel and that was that; suddenly I saw all organised religion as a bony bore, a monstrous fraud, a body of hypocrisy with no drop of living blood in its veins, no purpose in all its works. For some time there had been crystallising in my mind the proposition that prelates, politicians and actors all come out of the same egg-shell of vanity and that of the three of them the prelates, steeped in humbug, are the worst. As if sent to prove for me the truth of this theory there appeared on the religious front, in the usual three-year circuit which is common practice in Methodism, a reverend gentleman of unparalleled vanity, ill-manners and such a capacity for feeble sermonising that in adolescent outrage I quarrelled with him in a revolt the violence of which I have never regretted.

I will not go so far as to say that I never went to Chapel again. I went at least once, simply in order to appease Madge, who had been brought up as a Baptist, but so far had my contempt for organised religion advanced by that time that I spent the whole duration of the sermon reading a volume of Tchechov's stories thinly disguised between the covers of a hymn-book. The sowing of that particular handful of corn did, however, bear fruit. The next morning I sat down and wrote a story called, not inappropriately, *The Idiot*, the *genesis* of which had started in the middle of a hymn whose every word, like those of many more, I knew and still know by heart. I had now, in fact, reached the stage my grandfather had reached so long before me. He had long been sick of "popery, humbug and singing in night-shirts" and now I, on a parallel plane, but in a different faith, was sick too.

Some time before this my grandmother, a long and cruelly tortured sufferer from asthma, had died. My fondness for her and fear of her recurrent spasms of illness had led me to read Culpepper, whose herbal had long been treasured in the household. In the course of so doing I discovered that asthma, in company with some twenty other ailments ranging from ague to stone-in-the-kidneys, would yield to a concoction largely compounded of the roots of elm trees, boiled. I duly boiled some. They were very little roots, having been torn up with my bare hands from suckers springing up from trees large and mature and I boiled them for hours, to my mother's continued vexation, on the gas-stove in the kitchen. The resultant fluid, when strained, was a kind of litmus pink and thickish, like bad tomato ketchup. I longed desperately to create with it, like some youthful witch-doctor, a miracle of a cure for the sufferings of my grandmother, but its efficacy as a medicine was never tested. Both in consistency and colour it grew thicker and thicker until finally, unpleasantly pungent, it was thrown away, leaving my faith in Culpepper much shaken too.

After the death of my grandmother it seemed to me that my grandfather was already a breaking, if not broken, man. We are accustomed to think of the

Victorians as stuffy, tedious, strait-laced, cocooned in piety. It is my own conviction that they were by no means to be despised; they were hard-working, dedicated, inventive, even courageous. It required a brave man, I have always thought, to start out in mid-life, as my grandfather had done, to conquer with nothing but wheelbarrow, spade, fork and hoe a piece of English earth that would, in the course of time, go far towards killing him. In these days, when men not infrequently draw money for not working and when trade-unionese is the language used in talks arranged, in industrial disputes, to begin talks, it seems lunatic to a point of near-fantasy to think of a single-handed farmer toiling twenty summer hours a day with a half-broken down pony to extract a bare living from the soil and at the same time to retain a dignity, a purpose and a pride in the land.

In due course, in the late twenties, the land grew too much for him. *Thou thy worldly task has done, home art gone and taken thy wages* — the task was certainly done, the wages, in the form of a pension, were pretty meagre. Now, however, instead of struggling with plough and harrow over the intractable valley clay, while I harnessed the pony, mixed the pig-swill or dropped seed-potatoes into newly opened furrows, we were able to go about on more leisurely business, gathering watercress, fishing, black-berrying, gathering herbs, such as hounds-tongue, for some ointment in which he still had undiminished faith, sometimes even making toffee. I found time to walk with him a good deal and one of my favourite walks was down an ancient cow-trodden lane bearing the regal name of King's Meadow Lane and which led eventually to the Nene. There seems little doubt that the Romans trod this lane and perhaps grew, in a field beside it still called Vine Hills, their grapes. Tall bushes of misty-purple sloes (slons in the particular dialect of that part of the Midlands) almost met overhead; there was a great richness, in due season, of dog-roses and hawthorn, meadowsweet, kingcup and willow-herb.

When we finally paused at the bridge over the river it was to look out on a valley unenriched except at hay-time, when the thick deposits of silt left by winter flood-waters made every meadow a cornucopia and sometimes even led to the miracle of hay-harvest all over again in September. The Nene Valley at this point has none of the idyllic lusciousness of the Ouse but it was still not too late to see an occasional horse-drawn coal barge being drawn slowly downstream past the ruined *Wharf Inn*, where on the Victorian Sundays of my grandfather's youth men got roaring drunk, fought, argued and even drowned themselves. The ruin today goes further. Gravel pits of vast size scar the valley's entire width and a procession of trucks lumbers away day after day, some of them bearing some prized mystic and newly-discovered element found in the gravel, richer than all the hay-fields of Edwardian days put together.

Long before this the hiring-fairs, the distribution of largesse and breakfast beer and the annual invasion of the Irish had disappeared, but one great event still remained: the Feast. What Wakes are to the English North, so Feasts are to the East English Midlands. No other day of the year, except Christmas Day, had the same rich inducements and excitements to offer as Feast Sunday. On the first Sunday of July there were celebrated — and I hope still are — no less than fifty of these Feasts, so that the day was called Big Feast Sunday. The dates of these Feasts, rigidly fixed, are closely tied to the Church and they remind me, in several ways, of the *Pardons* of Brittany. With the celebratory day fixed by the Church there grew up, over the centuries, the usual secular accompaniments: the coconut shies, the shooting galleries, hoop-las, helter-skelters, gingerbread, darts, roundabouts and spit-rock. In Brittany, at the many *Pardons*, they sell *pommes frites*, candy floss, knick-knackery of all kinds, hideously embellished models of the Crucifixion in plastic, religious relics, balloons and all the rest of it. "The people o' Dublin," says Captain Boyle in O'Casey's *Juno and the Paycock*, "think more o' Charley Chaplin and Tommy Mix than they do of S.S. Peter and Paul." And in the same fashion it is my guess that the people of Higham Ferrers, on the second Sunday in August, cared more for the beer in *The Green Dragon*, *The Griffin* and *The Chequers* than they ever did for the blessed Virgin to whom their Church is dedicated.

We awaited that day — and not only children but all grown-ups too — with a positive fever. The affair was a rite. It was truly a business of feasting. It was an occasion for dressing-up, beer-swilling, parading the streets, family re-unions, torchlight processions. I had often heard my grandfather speak of the public tumult that greeted the relief of Mafeking and I always fancied that Feast Sunday was the next best thing. We began, first of all, with an enormous midday dinner: roast fowls and stuffing, roast beef and Yorkshire pudding, plum pies, a plum pudding left over from Christmas. Not to have been present at this rite would have been the equivalent, in a Roman Catholic, to rejecting the Sacrament. The house always seemed full of strange relatives, even stranger visitors from remote villages, seen only once a year. A great succulence of roasting meat filled the air and we eventually fell to our plates like a flock of Sunday-dressed vultures, my grandfather choking over the ferocious hotness of his home-made horseradish sauce, my grandmother tucking furtive silver threepenny bits into dark wedges of Christmas pudding. Shame, I think, would have descended on any house that ever failed to provide a comparable feast. "Have some more, Albert," would be my grandfather's continual cry, "Go on, man, have some more," but my father, replete, would retreat in polite refusal. Not so a distant relative samed Sip. Fat as a sow in pig, slow of mastication, benign of countenance, hungry of eye, Sip had come to the Feast to eat his fill and, though ordinarily looking as if about to burst, did so with bland, solemn and determined justice.

The ritual of that day continued after a tea almost as large as dinner itself — masses of bread-and-butter, the bread brown, white and currant, scones, sponges, apricots, pineapple, jams of blackberry and plum, celery, cheese with both celery and cake — with a slow family procession to the market place. Everyone was dressed up: the women in long sweeping skirts and huge hats feathered or flowered and blouses with mutton-legged sleeves, the men in best suits and straw-hats and often with button-holes of carnations and even of big, purple shaggy asters: so that memory tells me that it all looked, by the time we reached the thronged area of *The Green Dragon* and the little, chestnut-shaded market square, like something medieval, a pageant, one of those pictures one sees of Merrie England. It was here, in 1793, that the celebrated diarist and traveller, the Hon. John Byng, later Viscount Torrington, stayed at *The Green Dragon* en route for the North (Breakfast 9d, Dinner 1/6, Wine 2/6, Brandy 3d) and after Sunday breakfast powdered his hair and repaired to church, where the reigning parson "drawled the prayers and delivered a sermon . . . about the Philistines and preached to us about the Pharisees. Some poor weak singing . . . most people slept at the sermon; I was often on the brink," after which he crossed the Nene to Artleborough (still so called in my boyhood), and not as now, Irthlingborough, and so on to Kettering and "cold Venison pastie; upon which and cold lamb, I supped with much relish."

Torrington's description of *The Green Dragon*, at which my grandmother before her marriage had been "in service", the superb west door of the church, "one of the most beautiful sculptur'd porches that can be seen", the Bede House and the delicate grammar school built by Chichele, prove that in appearance the small and ancient borough had changed little since the days of the French Revolution. A vanished world? — change and decay? "At the town's end they have, even with this week, demolish'd several upper windows, arches etc., of the old College." With melancholy Torrington went on to complain that "our grandfathers cared for nothing of this sort! My grandsons will have nothing to see".

Happily Torrington's pessimism was unjustified — it was still all there for me to see much as he had himself seen it on that hot Sunday in 1793. He could not of course have seen the fair as I saw it, with the great steam traction engines of brassy power (now so assiduously collected by enthusiasts of at least that part of a vanished world) and the switch-backs crazy with gay models of the new horseless carriages. But the sight of stalls selling spit-rock (so called, as I say, because the rock-maker spat on his hands before twisting and moulding the great bronze-cream ropes of sugar), brandy snaps, gingerbread and whelks, might just as easily have come from that world of his when brandy was a mere threepence a glass and parsons droned on and on much as they do today. He might have seen too the giggling boy-and-girl exchanges of confetti, the swing-boats, the fortune tellers, the wild man from Borneo, the bearded lady and the tricksters selling this and that bargain to the gaping country crowds. What he certainly couldn't have seen was the new biograph in its dark sweaty tent, the new miracle of motion pictures, and above it all the splendour of the great church-spire, like an enormous inverted ice-cream cone, gleaming silver-gold in the reflection of electric light, gas-flares and paraffin lamps against the blue-black August sky.

In due course we played a sort of return match at Rushden on the first Sunday after the 19th of September, when our Feast too was celebrated, but the medieval air that still belonged to Higham Ferrers was never there. The town had no central market square; everything was more circumspect, more material, more scattered; the fair was held a mile from the church. Torrington would never have recognised the world of shoe factories and chapels, with not one parson but a dozen droning away at rival denominations Sunday after Sunday. It is true that we ate as well as at my grandfather's; the ladies' hats were still as large, the button-holes of asters and carnations still as flamboyant and ostentatious, but it was never, never quite the same. Among the pear-leaves turning purest copper and gold in the garden there was also always an air of sadness. Summer was ending; and there was an old saying "The Feast is over. Now you can shut the back door and claim (I suppose truthfully acclaim) winter."

Winter having been claimed, there was nothing much more of excitement in Higham Ferrers, in those early days, until Christmas, except harvest-home suppers, the inauguration of a new Mayor and the pot-cart. It says much for the character of these Edwardian autumns and winters that news of the arrival on the Market Square of a man selling from a horse-drawn wagon a load of cheap tea-services, dinner plates, wash-basins and ewers and chamber-pots should have spread about the town like news of the Battle of Waterloo. Even Rushden had its pot-cart, just as it now had its first semi-vaudeville, semi-cinema picture house at which Chaplin appeared both in person and on the screen. The days of the travelling penny gaff, presenting *Maria Martin* and so on, all the winter entertainment my grandfather ever knew except a rare night excursion or two to London to see Irving in Shakespeare, were long since over.

Now on winter evenings I often walked over the hill that separates the two towns and took my grandfather an ounce or two of tobacco or a few peppermints, generally known as "stripes", and played dominoes with him in front of the fire, under the black bars of which and above the gleaming steel fender a few potatoes were generally roasting for supper. With the gas-light glowing above the red chenille tablecloth and its pattern of black and white dominoes the scene must have looked very like one of those warm bourgeois family pieces so beloved and well recorded by Vuillard and Bonnard. By the time the old American clock on the wall, with its garish picture of the town of Philadelphia, had struck nine it was time for my grandfather to light a candle and go to bed.

To this scene I was determined to introduce Madge, reasoning that if my grandfather approved and liked her all would be well. To my great delight he liked her instantly. The fact that she was, as he said, "Higham Ferrers born-and-bred" was another point immensely in her favour; people who had been born otherwise were slightly beyond the pale. His pride and interest in the old town was in fact immense and as he learned that she too had been born a native of it he immediately wanted to know where?

"In one of those little thatched cottages under the walnut tree," she said — a walnut tree of immense size and age, sometimes alleged to have been planted in the reign of Henry VIII, stood at the bottom of the street, close by the farm where my grandfather had regularly failed to drink his pint of breakfast beer in his boyhood — "the second one from the top."

"Dall it, that's the house I was born in too," he said, greatly marvelling, and it was as if they were both, and always had been, of the same family.

I was now twenty. As 1925 came to an end I was still unemployed, still on the dole. I had now written not only novels, short stories and poems but also plays, mostly one-act plays, into one of which, *The Last Bread*, I had caustically poured some of my bitterness about the post-war twenties, not having read Knut Hamsun's *Hunger* for nothing. Of all these efforts not one had attracted a whisper of success. *The Two Sisters* was now with a tenth publisher. Not only did it seem that I had failed in my burning intentions to be a writer — a certain impatience in my character clearly led me to expect too much and too soon — but in the world of factories and chapels I still knew scarcely a soul with whom I could exchange a word on writing and literature.

Nevertheless there were certain compensations. I hadn't been to Cambridge; instead I had been to a University of my own, both as taught and teacher, undergraduate and tutor. I have been told that I learned to write much as Renoir learned to paint — *au musée*. However that may be it has always seemed to me that, left to my own resources, I discovered much about writing that no orthodox seat of learning could have taught me. Unguided, I had done a long, hard stint as undergraduate, alone. Now I was about to graduate.

A few days before Christmas, 1925, there arrived for me a letter from a firm of publishers, Jonathan Cape, lately of No. 11 Gower Street, now the home of *The Spectator*, but recently moved to more elegant premises at No. 30 Bedford Square.

In their letter they expressed their great interest in *The Two Sisters*. They liked it and wished to publish it. They also wished to meet me and wanted me, in turn, "to meet our reader", whose name was not disclosed. They were prepared to offer me a contract for the book and the sum, in advance of royalties, of £25.

It was a fortune. I was so excited that I took little notice of the fact that I had been addressed in the letter as "Dear Miss Bates": an enigma which needs, and will get, a solution later. All that seemed to matter, in that utterly unexpected event, was well expressed in Lawrence's words — "Look! We have come through."

ISIS publish a wide range of books in large print, from fiction to biography. A full list of titles is available free of charge from the address below. Alternatively, contact your local library for details of their collection of ISIS large print books.

Details of ISIS complete and unabridged audio books are also available.

Any suggestions for books you would like to see in large print or audio are always welcome.

ISIS

7 Centremead
Osney Mead
Oxford OX2 0ES
(01865) 250333

ISIS REMINISCENCE SERIES

The ISIS Reminiscence Series has been developed with the older reader in mind. Well-loved in their own right, these titles have been chosen for their memory-evoking content.

FRED ARCHER
The Cuckoo Pen
The Distant Scene
The Village Doctor

BRENDA BULLOCK
A Pocket With A Hole

WILLIAM COOPER
From Early Life

KATHLEEN DAYUS
All My Days
The Best of Times
Her People

DENIS FARRIER
Country Vet

WINIFRED FOLEY
Back to the Forest
No Pipe Dreams for Father

PEGGY GRAYSON
Buttercup Jill

JACK HARGREAVES
The Old Country

ISIS REMINISCENCE SERIES

MOLLIE HARRIS
A Kind of Magic

ANGELA HEWINS
The Dillen

ELSPETH HUXLEY
Gallipot Eyes

LESLEY LEWIS
The Private Life Of A Country House

JOAN MANT
All Muck, No Medals

BRIAN P. MARTIN
Tales of the Old Countrymen
Tales of Time and Tide

VICTORIA MASSEY
One Child's War

JOHN MOORE
Portrait of Elmbury

PHYLLIS NICHOLSON
Country Bouquet

GILDA O'NEILL
Pull No More Bines

VALERIE PORTER
Tales of the Old Country Vets
Tales of the Old Woodlanders

ISIS REMINISCENCE SERIES

ANIMALS

DAVID ATTENBOROUGH
Zoo Quest to Guyana

ALAN COREN
Animal Passions

MONICA EDWARDS
The Cats of Punchbowl Farm

PAUL HEINEY
Pulling Punches
Second Crop

PETER IRESON
Guiding Stars

SARAH KENNEDY
Terrible Pets

GLENDA SPOONER
For Love of Horses

ELISABETH SVENDSEN
Down Among the Donkeys
For the Love of Donkeys

ELIZABETH MARSHALL THOMAS
The Tribe of Tiger